IMAGES
of America

HIGHLAND
PARK

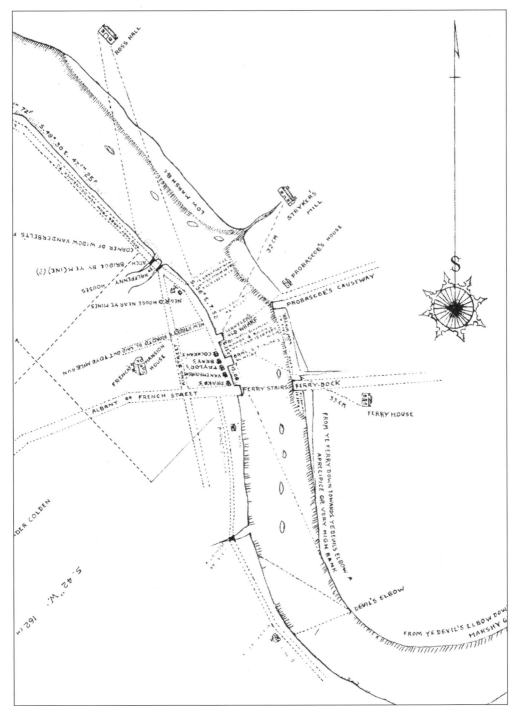

FRENCH'S PATENT OR MANNING'S SURVEY, 1790. This is one of the earliest maps detailing New Brunswick (on the left) and the area that would become Highland Park (on the opposite side of the Raritan River). The map locates Stryker's Mill on the Mill Brook, John Inian's ferry landings, and further downstream, the curve in the Raritan River named the "Devil's Elbow," which forms the borough's southern boundary. (New Brunswick Free Public Library.)

2

IMAGES
of America

HIGHLAND PARK

Jeanne Kolva and Joanne Pisciotta
for the Highland Park Historical Society

ARCADIA

Copyright © 1999 by Highland Park Historical Society.
ISBN 0-7524-1303-1

Published by Arcadia Publishing,
an imprint of Tempus Publishing, Inc.
2 Cumberland Street
Charleston, SC 29401

Printed in Great Britain.

Library of Congress Catalog Card Number: 99-62634

For all general information contact Arcadia Publishing at:
Telephone 843-853-2070
Fax 843-853-0044
E-Mail sales@arcadiapublishing.com

For customer service and orders:
Toll-Free 1-888-313-2665

Visit us on the internet at http://www.arcadiapublishing.com

Cover Photograph: Details on p. 114.

A TEENAGER RIDES TO SCHOOL, 1881. Condit Sniffen Atkinson rode his velocipede to Rutgers Preparatory School from his home in Spotswood. In 1893, he became editor of New Brunswick's *Daily Fredonian* newspaper, and by 1896 he was publisher and co-proprietor. During his long residency at 117 Benner Street, he held several positions including secretary of the New Brunswick Chamber of Commerce and district clerk for the Highland Park Board of Education. (The Atkinson Family.)

CONTENTS

THE TEN EYCK DAIRY AND COAL YARD, 1910. Important local businesses were featured in a border of buildings around Hughes and Bailey's 1910 Aero-View Map of New Brunswick. Located at 217 Harrison Avenue, W.W. Ten Eyck's dairy plant and coal yard was one of four Highland Park businesses represented. (Library of Congress Geography and Map Division.)

ACKNOWLEDGMENTS

We would like to express our gratitude to our donors, for without them, this book could not have materialized. We acknowledge each contributor by naming the source in parentheses after each caption. We would also like to thank the following people and organizations who lent their support in other essential ways: the original members of the Borough's Historical Commission; the Public Library staff; the Rutgers University Librarians at Alexander's Special Collections, including Albert C. King, Bonita Grant, Jim Robinson, Jan Riemer, and Ed Skipworth; Valerie Drach Weidmann; Ken Coster; Judy Kolva; Marie Vajo; Ruth Jansyn; Valerie Thompson; Bernice Bernstein; Gerta Klaus; Ira Susswein; Frank Conover; Reverend Richard Blake; Catherine Bull; Bill Callahan; Ellen Rebarber; Elizabeth Edgar; Audrey Messeroll; Mitch Dakelman; William Ducca; Lois Lebbing; Dorothy and Jerome Miller; Ruth Patt; Bert Freese; Bea Howley; Peter Primavera; Robin French; and our good luck charm, Juanita Barlow Messer. We would also like to thank those members of the Historical Society who have been vocally enthusiastic. Finally, to our families, thanks for your interest and support.

INTRODUCTION

In this book we offer a look at the growth of a town in the 19th and 20th centuries that had its humble start 300 years ago along the Lenape Indian's Assunpink Trail. European settlers transformed the trail into their main road connecting developing towns and cities through the eastern woodlands. As the Upper Road and Post Road, it eventually became the most important artery between New York and Philadelphia with its route through Highland Park and New Brunswick. Highland Park, well situated on the eastern bank of the Raritan River, has been connected to the commercial and industrial center of New Brunswick via ferry and bridge since 1685. One of the first commuting suburbs in the state, it arose consciously accommodating this different type of traveler. In the 18th century, pedestrians joined the horse-and-buggy traffic along the roadways. In the 19th and 20th centuries, modern trolleys, trains, and buses became viable commuting vehicles. Although automobiles now control New Jersey's thoroughfares, Highland Park remains a locus for pedestrians.

Throughout the 1800s, Highland Park's large farmland and wooded tracts were parceled off, as "East New Brunswick" became an attractive locale for the estates of upper-class, Anglo-Saxon descendants. It was during the 20th century that suburban housing developments would supplant these large land holdings. Today, only the river-view properties of the Cenacle Retreat House (Belleview), the Waldron House, and the former Meyer-Rice Estate (now the YM-YWHA) remain as vestiges of this by-gone era when huge estates encompassed the wooded bluffs.

Developing its own small-town identity slowly, in 1905 the Borough of Highland Park separated from Raritan Township (now Edison), which had been created from parts of Woodbridge and Piscataway Townships in 1870. Like many other small towns with similar patterns of development in the great Boston to Washington megalopolis, Highland Park's farmlands and single ethnic identity are long gone. An expanse of fruit orchards reaching to the river's edge no longer exists. With the internationally known Rutgers University nearby and the post-war construction of large apartment complexes, a population of great ethnic diversity today makes Highland Park a truly multi-racial and multi-ethnic community.

Compiling this book has been a labor intensive, yet rewarding, experience. Our approach was rather circuitous. We had a great desire to illustrate particular historical facts and attempted to locate images to support them. In some cases we were successful, in others not. We began with the Highland Park Historical Commission's collection of photographs. Word-of-mouth networking resulted in community groups and individuals coming forward. Some offered entire albums, others a precious snapshot or graphic. Discoveries of Highland Park-related images in library archives accelerated. The number of images began to grow and the problem soon became not too little material, but too much. Difficult choices had to be made.

Although we have presented many little-known facts of our town's history, there are many visual records not included here. The Airdome on River Road, Lydall's Needleworks, trotters at the race track, Forest Park's Ferris wheel, the interior of the movie theater, and the many gracious houses that lined Raritan Avenue and greeted visitors crossing the Albany Street Bridge are among the ones we were unable to locate. We hope these missing photographs do exist and are safely locked away in personal photo albums and that one day, they may surface to be shared with the general public. Finally, we ultimately hope that this collection of images will prompt the writing of an inclusive town history before the borough's centennial in the year 2005.

The Highland Park Historical Society seeks to promote the maintenance and rehabilitation of the town's historical resources, and to heighten awareness of the borough's historical and cultural heritage. Communications are welcomed and can be sent to P.O. Box 4255, Highland Park, New Jersey, 08904.

— Jeanne Kolva and Joanne Pisciotta

CAN SADIE COME OUT AND PLAY? In 1910, Sadie Hurlbut (first girl on the left) posed with her friends Walter Conover (standing behind post), Myrtle Ten Eyck (center), and Helen and Grace Conover (two on the right) on the porch of the old Hurlbut House, which was once located at 49 River Road. (Borough of Highland Park Historical Commission.)

One

BEFORE 1905

FRANK AYRES WORKS THE LAND, C. 1920. Frank Ayres is seen here working the fertile land of the Raritan River flood plain that he purchased in 1899. His property and the neighboring Donaldson Farm were converted into Middlesex County's Donaldson Park after WWII. (Highland Park Historical Society.)

THREE CENTURIES OF STEWARDSHIP, 1909. Belleview, Highland Park's oldest house, was built on land that once held Dr. Henry Greenland's late-17th-century inn. A portion of this house might be part of that original building. Situated along the Mill Brook section of the Lenape Indian's Assunpink Trail, the rural tract has had a succession of stewards including Robert Wood Johnson Jr., whose family owned the property from 1900 to 1950. This drawing, by J.H. Bailey & Co., places the house in its rural setting. (Borough of Highland Park Historical Commission.)

POSTCARDS AND COURTSHIP, C. 1906. To write to his sweetheart, Elizabeth Malmros, future mayor Edwin W. Eden used a postcard of Johnson's Pond. The pond was created by a dam on the Mill Brook that was raised an additional 4 feet in 1837, and its overflow powered a gristmill. Running parallel to and just north of the railroad tracks, the pond water also refilled steam engine tanks. In the 1900s, it was popular for both ice skating and swimming until it was drained in the 1940s, when Camp Kilmer was constructed. (Douglas Eden.)

FROM MANOR ESTATE TO SUBURB, C. 1905. The old Livingston Manor House at 81 Harrison Avenue remains Highland Park's most prominent river-view estate. In the early 19th century, this Greek Revival house was built upon a 151-acre property. It received its name after the president of Queen's College, Reverend John H. Livingston, bought it in 1809. Sold ten years later, a smaller 97-acre estate returned to the extended family's holdings in 1843 when the Reverend's nephew, Robert James Livingston, purchased the property. In 1890, a reporter claimed that the property was surrounded with a rustic fence made of branches that spelled out "Livingston" along its northern face. Shrinking in acreage with every sale, in 1897 the John Waldron Company bought a plot and Watson Whittlesey purchased the remaining tract for his future housing development. The house is pictured here before it received Whittlesey's Colonial Revival embellishments of a portico and enclosed side porch. The imposing house became his home and the Livingston Manor Corporation's sales office. Transferring hands once again in 1909, John Waldron bought the mansion on its relatively small plot as a wedding gift for his son and daughter-in-law, Eleanor. The house has remained in the Waldron family throughout the 20th century. (Alexander Library Special Collections and University Archives.)

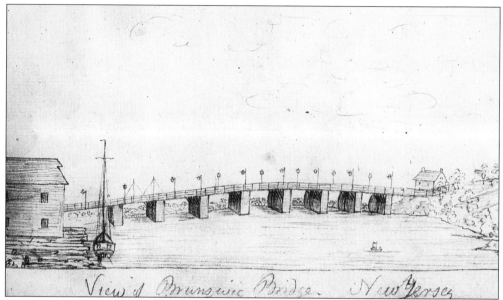

THE FIRST ALBANY STREET BRIDGE, 1795. When it first opened, Thomas Russell sketched the "Brunswick Bridge" that replaced Inian's Ferry and a fellow traveler, Isaac Weld, wrote about "the very neat and commodious wooden bridge that had been thrown across the Raritan River." Built by the New Brunswick Bridge Company, it became the most important component for local and regional transportation. Until noon on July 3, 1875, the moment Middlesex County made it toll free, several private companies owned, maintained, and rebuilt the bridge. (The Historical Society of Pennsylvania.)

"VIEW FROM RAILROAD HOTEL AT EAST NEW BRUNSWICK," C. 1838. Soon after the first railroad bridge, designed by Thomas Hassard, connected "East New Brunswick" to New Brunswick, J.H. Bufford created this lithograph "from nature and on stone." Trouble was inevitable for the double-decker bridge. In 1848, the county court charged the New Jersey Railroad and Transportation Company with inexcusable neglect, having failed to provide signals to forewarn the travelers in horse-drawn buggies below. The wooden structure burned down on March 9, 1878. (Alexander Library Special Collections and University Archives.)

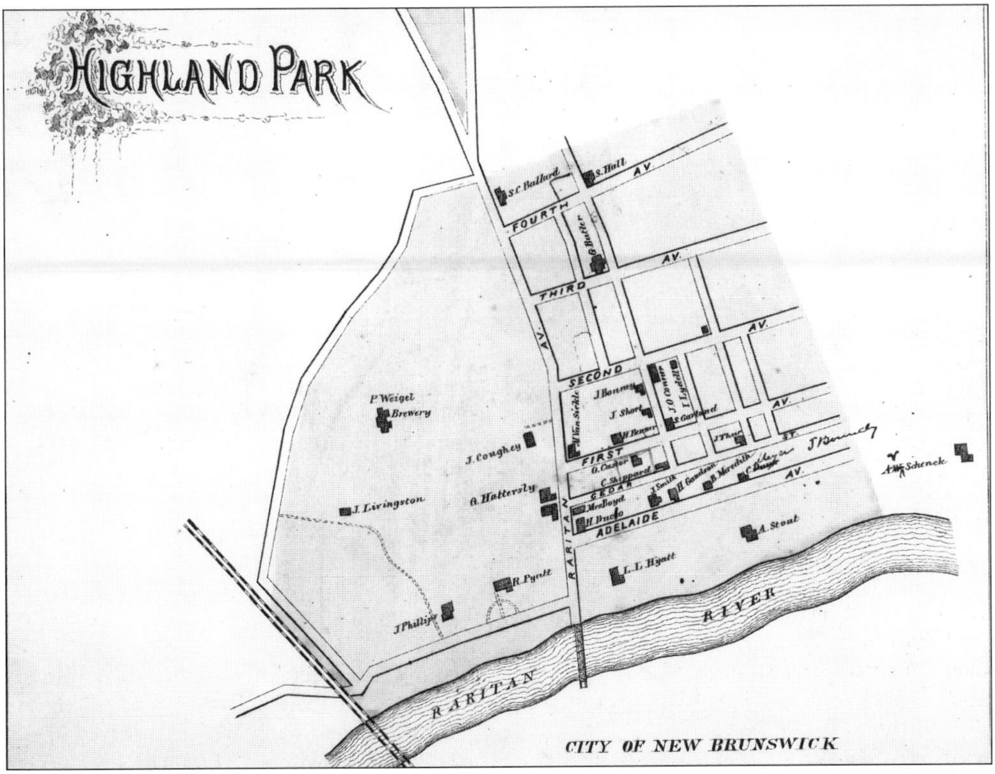

"A Tidy Little Package," 1876. In their 1876 map, Everts and Stewart recorded 28 residences of the "Highland Park" section of Raritan Township. Although the mapmakers missed several outlying houses in this small hamlet, 19 were mapped on the south side's grid-pattern streets to the right of Raritan Avenue, while the north side (to the left of the avenue) shows its large estates and the brewery. (New Brunswick Free Public Library.)

JOSEPH SCHNEIDER,

STEAM BREWERY,

RARITAN ROAD,

EAST NEW BRUNSWICK, N. J.

Same Location, Different Names, 1888. Shortly after Philip Weigel's brewery was destroyed in an 1873 fire, it was rebuilt, for it appears on the 1876 map at the top of this page. The Raritan Brewing Company, owned by George W. Wiedenmeyer, opened in 1877. Ten years later, Joseph Schneider took over the brewery and later bought advertising space in the 1888 New Brunswick Directory, shown here. By 1896, the business was run by the Waldschloss Brewing Company. Two years later, John W. Russert changed its name to the Rock Spring Brewery; by the 1900s its name had changed once again, this time to the New Brunswick Brewing Company.

ALEXANDER MERCHANT'S 1888 MAP. Listing over 70 residences and the occupants' names, this map is a valuable reference for the history of Highland Park's 19th-century families. Drawn from memory years later, the local architect recorded the town's cluster of houses along Raritan Avenue and south-side streets, and the outlying farms to the north, east, and south. The map lends credence to Reverend Thompson's 1891 statement, "We have all the rural beauty heart can wish. Add to this that Highland Park has the advantage of the city, and what more can a mortal desire?" As drawn here, the old Mill Road makes a grand westward sweep toward River Road from the intersection of the Woodbridge and Metuchen Roads. In 1836, the impassable railroad diverted it from its original course to the other side of the Mill Brook. (Borough of Highland Park Historical Commission.)

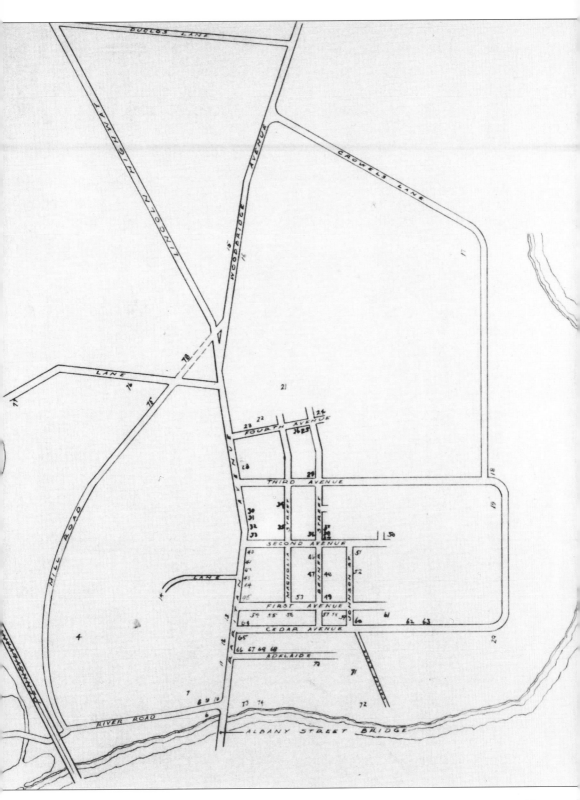

15

A FAMILY PORTRAIT, C. 1896. Early photography required long, motionless poses. The Barlow family's three generations did their best as they gathered in front of their Woodbridge Avenue farmhouse (#15, 1888 map). The Barlows are a good example of hard-working people who managed small businesses while living as an extended family under one roof. The house's age was not known, but family legend had it as one of George Washington's headquarters. It stood near South Tenth Avenue before being demolished in the 1960s. (Juanita Barlow Messer.)

THE LUCAS FARMSTEAD, 1942. When the owner of this house, Fielding G. Lucas, died in 1936 at the age of 91, he was New Jersey's only surviving Confederate veteran. Moving to Highland Park just after the Civil War, he acquired the Merrill farm, which had been established in 1745 near the intersection of today's Raritan and Woodbridge Avenues (#78, 1888 map). An 1890 directory lists Lucas as a lumber dealer, and in 1905 he became the borough's first marshal. This memorable farmhouse was replaced by a new public library in 1959. (Alexander Library Special Collections and University Archives.)

"ROMANTICALLY SITUATED STONE MANSION," 1907. So an author declared in 1873 about the 1855 Redcliffe Manor House (#72, 1888 map). Hidden among the cedars, it became the river-view home of New Brunswick Mayor Abraham V. Schenck, and remained in the family for many decades. By 1919, the estate became the Redcliffe Manor School, an outdoor school for well children. From 1923 to 1945, the Redcliffe Boarding House was run by Emily B. and Edith M. Schenck. The house was eventually demolished and a post-war apartment complex covered the hill top property. (Borough of Highland Park Historical Commission.)

Adelaide Avenue, Highland Park, N.J.

EARLY SUBURBANIZATION. This 1907 postcard offers a view of Highland Park's first tree-lined, suburban street. By 1850, Luke C. Coe's plots, once part of the Van Horne estate, appealed to wealthy urban businessmen who built their elegant residences along South Adelaide Avenue. Developers Hiram and Wesley Benner continued Coe's development by buying and selling lots earmarked for residential housing. The area was then alternately called "Raritan Park" or "Highland Park." By the 1870s, although it was a public street, South Adelaide Avenue had a gated entrance. (Borough of Highland Park Historical Commission.)

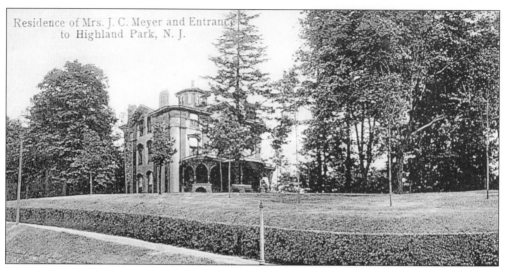

Residence of Mrs. J. C. Meyer and Entrance to Highland Park, N. J.

"ONE OF THE MOST ELEGANT RESIDENCES," 1910. Known as the Meyer-Rice estate in the 1900s, this Italianate mansion near the Albany Street Bridge cuts a fine silhouette atop a high bluff overlooking the Raritan River. Originally owned by William Reed in the 1860s, it had a succession of owners until its sale to the Young Men's, Young Women's Hebrew Association in 1955. Now surrounded by a 40,000-square-foot recreational facility, the old mansion is home to the children who attend the YM-YWHA's preschool. (Carolyn Kuhlthau.)

THE MEYER FAMILY PREPARES FOR AN OUTING, C. 1897. Posing for New Brunswick photographer Isaac S. Van Derveer, Kate Davison Meyer sits next to the driver while her two sisters (wearing the big hats), her two daughters, and her son ride in the back of the carriage. John Christopher and Kate D. Meyer bought the house in 1883, but tragically, Mr. Meyer died at the age of 44, only five years later. Throughout the 19th century, the Meyer family's fortune was amassed from their business of binding cloth to rubber. They owned factories in both New Brunswick and Milltown. (Borough of Highland Park Historical Commission.)

TODAY'S ALBANY STREET BRIDGE, 1892. Rendered in brushed ink on paper by an anonymous painter, this sketch offers a look at early construction practices. Another eye-witness was longtime Highland Park resident and apprentice mason William U. Selover, who wrote in his diary on July 22, 1892, that "I worked some on the Albany St. bridge arches—11 skewbacks thick—but found the work too hard." The bridge, completed in 1893, came none too soon for travelers, who once again had been ferried across the wide river. (Alexander Library Special Collections and University Archives.)

"ALL ABOARD" C. 1909. This trolley serviced Highland Park as it coursed between Perth Amboy and New Brunswick. First opened in 1897, the Brunswick Traction Company laid its "electric road" along Raritan Avenue. Taken over by the Middlesex & Somerset Traction Company in 1900, several years later the expanded lines were run by the Public Service's Central Division. The last line closed in 1937. A trolley to Bound Brook ran along River Road and the track's right-of-way is still visible in the area of Johnson Park. (Bill Christian.)

BELLS RING AT THE FIRST SCHOOLHOUSE, 1886. In 1885, Raritan Township allowed the formation of the Highland Park school district. This Queen Anne-style building, designed by George K. Parsell, opened on March 23, 1886, to the ringing of Lydall and Beekman's donated bell. Teacher Chrissie Bartle gladly relocated her class of 30 students from Dr. Chevalier's rented extension parlor at 233 Magnolia Street. To lessen outside disturbances in this stricter era, the windows were built 6 feet high off the floor. Two one-room additions were added to the school in 1890 and 1897. (Borough of Highland Park Historical Commission.)

ORIGINAL HOSE CART, C. 1904. In 1891, a bucket brigade was organized in Highland Park. Eight years later, a hose company was formed to fight fires and to help control the transients camped near Johnson's Pond. The hose company's first piece of equipment was this 1899 hand-drawn cart used to carry and lay the firehose. Despite its elegant design, the pump was too weak for major fires, and on several occasions the volunteers had to await the arrival of New Brunswick's steamer. (Ex-Fire Chief Gerard T. Schultz.)

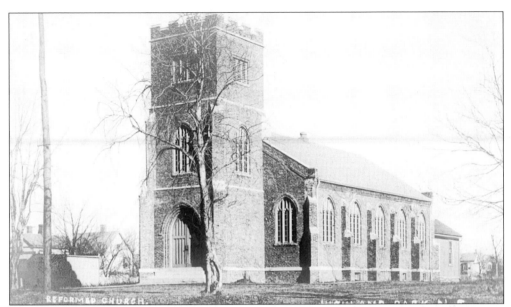

REFORMED CHURCH, 1901. On Thanksgiving Day, 1891, Reverend John Bodine Thompson referred to his Magnolia Street chapel as "the only church in the village." Between 1895 and 1896, Highland Park's first congregation enthusiastically raised money for their new church on South Second Avenue (pictured here). Designed by deacon Alexander Merchant, the cornerstone for the central tower church with its Gothic Revival windows was laid on October 3, 1897. It was dedicated exactly one year later. (Douglas Eden.)

MUSIC UP TO THE RAFTERS, 1904. The Reformed Church's interior with its dark wooden rafters was enhanced in part due to a matching grant from philanthropist Andrew Carnegie, who offered $500 if the congregation could raise the same amount. Subsequently, a pipe organ was installed in the summer of 1904. By this time, the congregation had grown significantly from its 20 founding families. After the church's construction, it was also used for secular gatherings. Raritan Township's Highland Park District School commencement took place here in June of 1900. (Douglas Eden.)

IRON TRUSS RAILROAD BRIDGE, 1878–1902. In the first of a series of four photographs captured on glass plates, perhaps by John W. Hurlbut, a steam engine pulls a heavy load of boxcars and hopper cars laden with coal away from industrial New Brunswick. This railroad bridge replaced a temporary structure that had been erected to keep the trains moving after the double-decker bridge burned down in 1878. The modern, iron truss structure carried regional freight traffic in the last quarter of the 19th century. (Marion Flomerfelt.)

ENGINEERING MARVELS, 1902. In 1902, New Brunswick Common Council passed an ordinance that allowed the Pennsylvania Rail Road to elevate its tracks through the city requiring a higher bridge over the Raritan to match the newly raised tracks. Chief Engineer William H. Brown designed a majestic stone arch bridge of 21 spans and work was begun on widening the piers to support it. Train traffic was not disturbed during this major project. Half of the new arches were constructed alongside the iron truss bridge after it was shifted over 14 feet on May 26, 1902, in front of a huge gathering of onlookers. (Marion Flomerfelt.)

MONUMENTAL SCALE, 1902. The workmen on top create a human scale with which to compare the enormous size of these new archways. Here, part of the trestle has been removed and the second half of the arches are under construction. Travelers still pass through this archway on the bike path that parallels River Road in Highland Park. (Marion Flomerfelt.)

LOOKING LIKE A ROMAN AQUEDUCT, 1903. Still serving the Northeast Corridor with its four tracks, the Pennsylvania Rail Road has long been crucial for the region's industrial and commercial expansion. Barge traffic on New Brunswick's Raritan-Delaware Canal declined but rail commuters contributed to the suburban growth of the 1900s. Completed in 1903, sections of the stone arch bridge were covered with concrete during the 1940s. Nevertheless, it remains an impressive testament to modern engineering. (Marion Flomerfelt.)

y. DARK - VIEW FROM ROOF "BUTLER'S HOUSE"

LOOKING BACKWARD, 1902. In his diary so titled, William U. Selover confessed that in school he was "not good at letters." Over a century later, he is being proved wrong. Selover moved to 215 Magnolia Street as a ten year old in 1876. His later blue-collar jobs included work at Lydall's Needleworks for $3 to $5 per week and construction on the 1897 schoolhouse addition. After buying a camera in 1900, he recorded the open fields between his house and the neighboring "Buttler House." (Alexander Library Special Collections and University Archives.)

1904

MOTHER IN HER GARDEN, 1904. In his illustrated diary, Selover also included this picture of Elizabeth Selover taken in the garden behind the mansard house still on Magnolia Street. Commenting on modern progress in 1901, he conjured up beautiful 19th-century imagery when he wrote, "the arc lights are now on Raritan Ave—how dark it used to be when we hung out the lantern to light father home and listened for the horses' feet in the alley." (Alexander Library Special Collections and University Archives.)

THE DEL VALLE HOUSE, 1875. Here is a closer view of the Italianate-style "Buttler House" that once stood at the corner of South Third Avenue and Benner Street. By 1899, the house was owned by capitalist Fernando Del Valle and his wife, Natividad, who lived there until 1936. Known as the Del Valle House after the 1930s, it was demolished and the Magnolia Garden Apartments were built on its land. (Borough of Highland Park Historical Commission.)

OFFICIAL PROGRAM

RARITAN DRIVING ASSOCIATION

RACE MEETING

DECORATION DAY
Friday, May 30, 1902

HIGHLAND PARK, NEW BRUNSWICK, N. J.

☞ Number on driver's arm corresponds with horse's number on program.

PRICE, TEN CENTS

A FLEETING GLANCE. This 1902 program is a great souvenir of the racetrack that once stood along Woodbridge Avenue between South Eleventh Avenue and Duclos Lane. Gala harness races and horse shows took place several times a year from 1900 until 1906. The local youths helped take care of the trotters from all over the state. On May 30, 1907, a bright-lights amusement park called Electric Park opened for the season on the flat tract of land that several years later would see the building of the neighborhood nicknamed the RaceTrack district. (A private collection.)

FIRST MAYOR AND COUNCIL, 1905. On March 15, 1905, Highland Park officially became a separate borough, seceding from Raritan Township. The drive was motivated by the high taxes paid to the township with little benefit returning to Highland Park, and the desire for an independent school district. James B. Archer, a New Brunswick shoe merchant and South Adelaide Street resident, was elected mayor, winning many of the 150 votes cast. For this May 1, 1905 photograph, the new officials were seated on the porch of the old Venable House that once stood at 142 Raritan Avenue. All Democrats, they are, from left to right, as follows: (bottom row) Frank Metzrath, Charles Tamm, John S. Turner, William Redfield, George F. Eden, and James Jenkins; (top row) Alvin Randolph, Otto Lindner, Anthony J. Gebhardt, James B. Archer, William Donomore, and John E. Whitehead. Other borough officials not photographed were John W. Russert, Charles P. Page, and John Cordo. (Borough of Highland Park Historical Commission.)

Two

LABOR AND CAPITAL
BUILD THE TOWN

A VIEW TOWARD THE AVENUE, C. 1908. During the administration of mayor Lorenz Volkert from 1908 to 1914, secondary dirt roads on the north side of Raritan Avenue were mapped and graded. Here, Civil Engineer George W. Conover and an assistant survey the lane then called Highland Avenue. This view from Montgomery Street looking toward Raritan Avenue shows the backs of two prominent buildings along the horizon—the Baptist Chapel to the left of the intersection and the firehouse to the right. (Highland Park Reformed Church.)

A VIEW TOWARD THE MANOR, C. 1908. For several years, Highland Avenue was the main thoroughfare from Raritan Avenue into Watson Whittlesey's private Livingston Manor. Carrying telephone wires, these poles march past the Martin shanty and John H. Johnson's house. With only two other ways into this neighborhood, a steep road off of River Road and the old Mill Road from North Fifth Avenue, the tract remained rather secluded. In 1916, the company offered the private manor streets to become public ones. The borough council accepted the offer and renamed this road of egress, North Second Avenue. (Highland Park Reformed Church.)

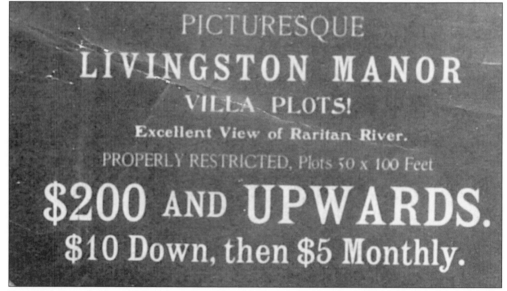

PICTURESQUE LIVINGSTON MANOR, 1909. Beginning in 1906, Watson B. Whittlesey, an innovative real estate developer, marketed his private Livingston Manor estate for suburban development. In one of the 20th century's earliest planned developments, lots were subdivided and sold with company constructed houses. Hawked via broadsides to New Brunswick's and New York City's white-collar workers, the houses upon these $200 "villa" plots reasonably cost $3,000 and up. (Borough of Highland Park Historical Commission.)

AN ARCHITECT'S HOME, 1933. Whittlesey was an architect from Rochester, New York, and was inspired to build himself this Mission Revival-style house on Harrison Avenue after a trip to California. It was built around an atrium and completed in 1911. On March 1 of that year, Whittlesey held a masquerade ball for 150 guests at a "big house-warming at the bungalow." The developer lived there only three years, for he died suddenly on April 7, 1914, at the age of 52. As his livelihood, J. Lloyd Grimstead sold many such photographic postcards to occupants in 1933. (Borough of Highland Park Historical Commission)

A NEIGHBORHOOD GROWS, 1910. By the time this Aero-View map detail was drawn, over three dozen houses and the field club were built. Longtime resident Carl Woodward recently stated that, "Livingston Manor was growing by leaps and bounds." By 1912, over 114 houses had been finished and occupied largely with Rutgers professors, business executives, merchants, and a few New York City commuters. Highlighting the distinction this district received, the 1911 Suburban Directory identifies all the Livingston Manor houses with individual numbers two years before the borough's system was officially adopted in 1913. (Library of Congress Geography and Maps Division.)

UNPAVED AVENUES, C. 1915. Mapping, grading, and curbing roadways seems to have been the borough's continuous responsibility from 1905 on. Unpaved roadways were made passable by loads of ashes and cinders. Town-wide paving with concrete and macadam began in the 1920s. As late as 1936, however, residents along sections of Harrison, Cleveland, and North Adelaide Avenues opted not to pay the special assessments that would come in exchange for paved streets. (Carolyn Kuhlthau.)

GRIMSTEAD REAL PHOTO POSTCARD, 1933. The Grimstead photograph collection of architectural portraits offers a look back to the time before air conditioning when many houses had striped canvas awnings and layers of lush landscaping to keep cool. This Livingston Manor house at 48 Grant Avenue shows both characteristics. (Borough of Highland Park Historical Commission.)

"A FINE PARK," 1933. One of the amenities of the Viehmann Tract was a park located on the property. A brochure advertises "wading, shady walks and rustic benches which make it an ideal resting spot." George A. Viehmann's "Colony of Homes" eventually covered the area between North Fifth and North Eleventh Avenues, from Raritan to South Park Avenues. Houses could be built based on buyer's sketches. Here Grimstead posed Alex Levin and his car in front of his "cozy home" at 27 North Sixth Avenue. (Borough of Highland Park Historical Commission.)

NORTH SEVENTH AVENUE, 1918. These young curbside saplings did not provide much shade, but then, raking leaves was easier in the fall. The Viehmann Tract's private park was at the far end of this Seventh Avenue view. In 1914, after several years of growth, the Viehmann Tract's convenient location next to the newly opened Lincoln Highway became one more selling point. In addition to its proximity to markets, churches, and schools, three trolley lines, including the Fast Line from Trenton to Newark, serviced the tract. (Carolyn Kuhlthau.)

PULLEYS AND METAL, C. 1922. With its great work force, the decade of the 1920s saw vast improvements to the town's infrastructure. Sidewalks were laid, and streets were graded and curbed. In 1928 alone, $250,000 was spent on new paving, water system extensions, storm drains, and sanitary sewers. At the corner of South Third Avenue and Benner Street, workmen used construction equipment that looks like large versions of children's metal Erector sets. An interested bystander and future mayor, Edwin W. Eden, most likely photographed this scene. (Douglas Eden.)

PAVING BENNER STREET, C. 1922. Benner Street was only one of a large number being paved during the 1920s. The 1930 census lists Highland Park's population at 8,739, and by then the town could boast about its 20 miles of concrete streets, an extraordinary amount for a borough of its size. Street names, which had been duplicated causing confusion and postal delays, were renamed. Community Night and Father-Son Week became important small-town events organized to bring together diverse groups of residents. (Douglas Eden.)

WIDENING THE ALBANY STREET BRIDGE, 1925. Created in 1914, the Lincoln Highway stretched from New York to San Francisco, passing through town along Raritan Avenue. Included in the Lincoln Highway Association archive, these two photographs depict the 1925 widening of the Albany Street Bridge and Raritan Avenue at the foot of the hill. Unfortunately, the improvements only added to the constant headache of unregulated traffic along this major thoroughfare. By 1928, Mayor Eden called the New York City buses "the worst offenders" and called for action against the "traffic evil" by instituting a campaign to curb reckless driving. Despite the presence of police officers wearing white storm coats, in 1929 there were over 170 accidents on Raritan Avenue. After traffic lights were installed one year later, the number dropped to 56. (University of Michigan at Ann Arbor.)

BUILDING BOOM, 1924. While Whittlesey and Viehmann were building houses on the north side, the south side also became the site of housing developments such as Riverview Terrace and Magnolia Heights. In 1926, there were 350 residential properties under construction in Highland Park. This house arose at 240 Magnolia Street and became Joseph and Ethel Barlow's home. (Juanita Barlow Messer.)

A NEW CHURCH RISES, 1926–27. Ground was broken in the fall of 1926 and by November 1927, the All Saints Episcopal Church at South Third Avenue and Benner Street was finished. Created through the efforts of two firms from Trenton, the P. J. Fowler Company designed the church and Thomas M. Day and Sons built it. Between 1913 and 1930, four churches and one synagogue were constructed in Highland Park. (Juanita Barlow Messer.)

A FAMILY ENDEAVOR, 1940. Development was slower on the south side to the east of South Sixth Avenue. Large expanses of wooded land from Woodbridge Avenue to the river are fondly remembered. These open spaces disappeared during the construction of apartment complexes in the 1950s. Beginning in the 1920s, Frank Pisciotta and his family built several houses on Karsey Street, including the one pictured here. From left to right are Frank Pisciotta Sr.; San Steffano, a friend; Frank's sons Richard, Carl, and Joe; and Joe's son Carl. (Joanne Pisciotta.)

MOVING DAY, C. 1948. Moving buildings, however commonplace in the past, was no small feat. Here, the Highland Park Diner is being positioned upon Felix Farenga's lot at the corner of South Seventh and Woodbridge Avenues. The building at the left, once a confectionery, served as the diner's kitchen. Carl Pisciotta, the diner's owner, was also Highland Park's building inspector during the late 1940s and 1950s. The diner operated until 1968, when it was demolished. (Felix Farenga.)

HIGH SCHOOL ADDITIONS, 1958. Construction machinery grew bigger as did Highland Park once again in the decades after the Second World War. Here, workmen begin the construction of the high school's science wing along North Fifth Avenue. (Bernice Bernstein Archive, Highland Park Historical Society.)

RIVERVIEW APARTMENTS, C. 1960. Flying high above Highland Park in Dr. Choper's airplane, photographer Joseph Koye made this portrait of the Redcliffe Apartments and the elegant homes along South Adelaide Avenue. Built on the Schenck property that once held the Redcliffe Manor House, the borough's first large, postwar apartment complex was completed by 1951. (Rich Odato.)

Three

MANUFACTURERS
AND MERCHANTS

THE MOST Sanitary and Up-to-date Clarifying, Pasteurizing and Bottling Plant.

Visitors Welcomed

W. W. TEN EYCK & SON

THE TEN EYCK DAIRY, 1910. William W. Ten Eyck (Dutch for "by the oak") started a dairy in 1886 with one Jersey cow. It produced five quarts of milk on the first day, which Ten Eyck dipped straight out of his pail. By 1917, the business was producing 3,000 quarts per day. He was the first in the area to sell milk in glass bottles, to pasteurize milk, and to make deliveries by automobile. Ten Eyck's addresses were 217 then 437 Harrison Avenue. After changing the business's name to the Highland Park Dairy in 1909, he changed it again in 1920 to Oakland Farms. (Lilian Handel.)

THE NEW BRUNSWICK BREWING COMPANY, 1908. The last of a long list of breweries, the New Brunswick Brewing Company had one of the first telephone numbers in Highland Park. An ill-fated business, there were numerous fires and even a 1903 murder committed by a hobo from the "tramp camp" during its long history. The brewery burned down on December 16, 1912, a decade ahead of Prohibition. Only the bottling department, a large, brick building, survived the inferno. It is now the apartment house at 105 Montgomery Street. (New Brunswick Directory, 1908.)

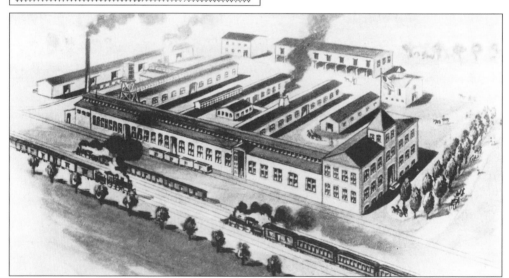

THE WALDRON MACHINERY COMPANY, 1907. "We brought the plant over here in 1897 and put it down in a cornfield," stated owner William Waldron in a 1927 interview. Thus, was established one of Highland Park's first major industries. Built on land between Cleveland Avenue and the railroad tracks, the factory produced the machines that were used to manufacture wallpaper, playing cards, and other paper goods. In 1926, it was listed as one of six town businesses with over one hundred employees. Surviving the Depression, by 1939 it had 170 employees. (Borough of Highland Park Historical Commission.)

1898–1948

A 50TH ANNIVERSARY PORTRAIT, 1948. They haven't lost their jobs! Three years after the end of World War II, many of Highland Park's women were still "manning" the J.S. Turner White Metal Company. Known as Turner Tubes, this plant was established in 1898 by John S. Turner and it manufactured collapsible tubes for holding creams and ointments. Johnson & Johnson was their first customer. Besides running the company, Turner, who had been on the first borough council, was active in both the fire department and the Democratic Party until his death in 1922. His children and grandchildren took over the business. The family lived in a house in front of the factory located at 220 Raritan Avenue. The business eventually relocated to South Brunswick, and in 1962 all but one of the buildings making up the factory complex were dismantled. (John E. Turner.)

AN OFFICIAL PORTRAIT, 1922. Lily Venable could be in this panoramic photograph. She is listed in a 1922 directory as a billing clerk for one of the largest manufacturers of wallpaper in the U.S., Janeway & Carpender, a company whose products were known worldwide. In its heyday, over 300 employees worked at the 6-acre Highland Park plant. Despite the photograph's inscription locating this company in New Brunswick, it was not. When the Janeway & Carpender Wallpaper factory in New Brunswick was destroyed by fire on March 13, 1907, a site was purchased in Livingston Manor from Whittlesey's Livingston Manor Corporation. Contracts were awarded for the building of a new plant before the end of the same

day. Located on Janeway Avenue, between Cleveland Avenue and the Pennsylvania Railroad, its tall water tower and smokestack changed the look of Highland Park's skyline. It was not a coincidence that its location was adjacent to Waldron's machine factory. Colonel Jacob James Janeway ran the business until his death in 1926. Janeway & Carpender had an additional appeal to the town's youngsters—there was a good field for playing ball behind the building and Janeway's whistle would blow loud and clear whenever school was canceled for the day. The stock market crash of 1929 decimated the wallpaper manufacturer, and in the spring of 1931 its doors were closed forever. (Borough of Highland Park Historical Commission.)

PORTRAIT OF A LEADER, 1920. In 1920, at the age of 26, Robert Wood Johnson Jr., son and nephew of the founders of Johnson & Johnson, became the town's youngest mayor after serving on the borough council. He became president of J&J in 1930 and successfully led the company with no loss of jobs through the Depression. He and his brother, John Seward Johnson, are credited with making the company an international one. A great philanthropist, he was also involved in local fund-raising efforts and celebrations. In 1955, he spoke at Highland Park's Golden Jubilee. He died at the age of 74 in 1968. (Borough of Highland Park Historical Commission.)

THE MUSTARD PLASTER FACTORY, 1901. Under the direction of William H. Johnson, mustard plaster bandages were manufactured in this building, one of nine J&J built in the 1890s. The factory was on land leased from Andrew J. Conover along today's Lincoln Avenue, halfway between Raritan Avenue and Montgomery Street (#7 on the 1888 map). Eventually J&J owned the property with its spring and reservoir. The stream's pure water, carried under the Raritan through pipes, was reserved for the laboratories in New Brunswick, where the company relocated all its operations after a fatal fire on February 2, 1917. (Borough of Highland Park Historical Commission.)

"MERRIEWOLD," C. 1975. The Kaplan Organization at 433 River Road has "the most unique business address in New Jersey" in their mansion, "The Castle." Resting on a wooded property that once consisted of 150 acres, Merriewold was constructed in 1926 from stone imported from England by J. Seward Johnson for his wife, Ruth. The 25-room mansion by New York architect Thomas H. Ellett features 11 fireplaces, over 150 leaded windows, and two spiral stairways. As if from the pages of British fiction, it became the site of an attempted kidnapping of the Johnson's daughter and later, under different ownership, the infamous Farmer murder. (The Kaplan Organization.)

KITCHENMEISTER FLORISTS, 1920. A family business in operation for 80 years is a rarity. In 1883, Edward Kitchenmeister started a florist shop in New Brunswick and purchased land bordered by the Mill Brook for his greenhouses and gardens. Surrounded by gardens, the Kitchenmeisters dubbed the property "Floral Valley." A photograph taken in the 1920s shows the dirt lane at the edge of Highland Park that would become North Fifth Avenue. In 1962, this family sold the business to another one who has carried on the tradition. (Gail Dimitri.)

THE AYRES FARMHOUSE AND ITS OWNER, 1922. The map of 1888 situates this farmhouse (#20) at the end of Cedar Avenue. By 1899, milkman Frank Ayres lived here. Running his successful business into the mid-1920s, Ayres owned a large tract of land bordered by Cedar and Riverview Avenues, and the Raritan River. He farmed the land by the river and delivered milk and cream to the scattered residents along a route that included Benner Street, Cedar, Raritan and South Adelaide Avenues, and streets in New Brunswick. His February 1907 record book kept track of regular deliveries, returned milk, and extra milk sold. A note reminded him that Mrs. Dodd wanted an additional 1/2 pint of cream on Thursday! He looks ready for a pleasure trip in the photo portrait below. (Highland Park Historical Society.)

AYRES BEACH, C. 1924. In the 1920s, Frank Ayres ran a private swimming beach and boat dock on his property abutting the Raritan River. According to longtime resident Herbert Meseroll, Frank's wife, Bertha Ayres, sold ice cream upstairs at the beachhouse. In this striking snapshot taken from a rowboat offshore, Highland Parkites enjoy themselves at their local beach. (Highland Park Historical Society.)

AYRES DRY DOCK, 1930. The Raritan River Boat Club was an active organization in the region and many owners repaired and stored their motor boats at Ayres Dry Dock. As the Raritan got too polluted for swimming, the popularity of boating began to rise. (Borough of Highland Park Historical Commission.)

45

"Toft's Hotel," c. 1911. Mayor James B. Archer referred to this local hotel as "Toft's Hotel" in 1905. Opened for business in 1897, the 20-room lodging at the crossroads of Woodbridge and Raritan Avenues had a succession of proprietors and managers, including Hans Toft and Rudolf Osterwald. Renamed the Highland Park Inn in 1909, it became the Highland Park Hotel once again in 1913. Celebrities associated with the hotel include the poet Joyce Kilmer, who frequented its beer garden, and Bibi Osterwald, the manager's daughter, who was a celebrated New York stage actress and singer from the mid-1940s to the 1970s. (Carolyn Kuhlthau.)

The Past Meets the Future, 1922. Three modes of transportation are depicted in this view along Raritan Avenue—an ox-drawn cart, trolley tracks, and new automobiles in the window. (Juanita Barlow Messer.)

ONE PUMP AT HODGES GARAGE, 1924. In 1914, the automobile census for the entire county counted only 1,600 cars. Gasoline and service stations such as Hodges' Garage at 10 North Second Avenue filled the need to keep the machines running. This building consisted of a first-floor garage and a large upper room that served as the Borough Hall from May 1920 until late 1923, in addition to being rented to other organizations such as the American Legion and the Trinity Church. Dash's TV repair shop and the B. Beamesderfer Art Gallery are its current occupants. (Phyllis Loetzer.)

A BUSINESS FOR GASOLINE, 1937. By the 1930s, pumping gas was no longer merely a sideline—the service station could stand as a business unto itself. Angelo Lenetti built his station at the corner of Woodbridge and South Eleventh Avenues. It was run by his two sons, Dominick and Frank, until 1976. Travelers along the nearby national highways could camp behind the station. The land seen on the right is Irving School's playground. (Mrs. Rosalie Lenetti.)

THE BANKING BUSINESS, 1924. Opened for business on December 1, 1924, at the Masonic Building, The First National Bank of Highland Park received these congratulatory bouquets from well-wishers. Highland Park's new bank offered the same services as New Brunswick's banks, such as Christmas Club savings plans and safety deposit boxes, although with the advantage of being closer to home. (Juanita Barlow Messer.)

GALA WEEK Starting July 5th GALA WEEK
Matinee Daily

Big Outdoor Attraction at

FOREST *Amusement* PARK

The Management Offers

F. V. Hocum's Super One-Ring Circus

10 People, 3 Horses, 6 Dogs, 1 Trick Mule and Several Doves

Change of Program Daily

FOREST PARK, 1921. Starting in the 1890s, the Aurora Singing Society held socials on their tract of land off Woodbridge Avenue along today's Aurora Street. By May 30, 1920, "Forest Park" opened as an amusement park with a dance hall and merry-go-round. Joining attractions such as this advertised circus, dances, sometimes featuring Broadway bands, were held year-round until 1925. Ladies paid 25¢ while gents shelled out 45¢, tax included. The dance hall was moved to 168 Woodbridge Avenue in 1926, and is today's Forrest Park Professional Building. (*Daily Home News*, July 7, 1921.)

OUR OWN MOVIE HOUSE, 1927. From 1927 until the late 1950s, Highland Park marginally supported a movie theater. With matinees costing adults 20¢ and children a dime, motion pictures were shown in the 1,400-seat playhouse along with "News Reels, Comedies and Novelties." After opening in 1927, Mark Block's theater, with its beautiful interior (including a fountain and an aquarium), tried but failed to stand up to the enforcement of New Jersey's Blue Laws, which barred businesses from operating on the Christian Sabbath, Sunday. (Eleanor Williams.)

FROM GROCER TO BARBER, 1930. Service businesses such as pharmacies and barber shops make small towns very comfortable places. Angelo Parlo was first a grocer from 1926 to 1930, and then a barber in the same shop at 106 Woodbridge Avenue. Here posing as customers are Nick Saltarella in the left-hand chair and John Parlo, Angelo's father, in the other one. Angelo's young son Jack, seen helping here, eventually came to own the shop in the 1960s. It then expanded to include the beauty salon of his wife, Rita. (Shear Expressions.)

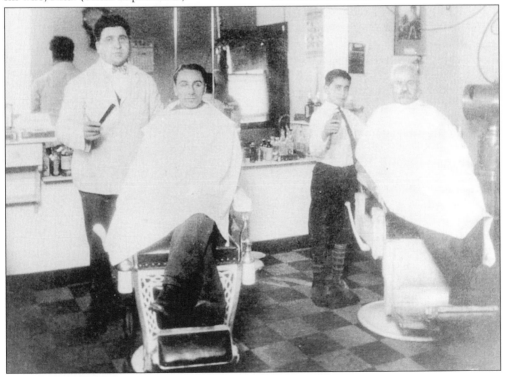

ESSENTIAL GROCERIES, 1953. Second graders from Irving School took a field trip to various local landmarks including the police station and post office, making a stop at the Acme Market on Raritan Avenue. By the 1950s, with a population over 10,000, the town could support major grocery chain stores. This did not mean the end of the smaller mom-and-pop grocery stores; they continued to thrive up and down the commercial district. (Joanne Pisciotta.)

FAMILY OF FLAKO PRODUCTS, 1954. Taken from an old recipe booklet, this Pop Art image contains the history of a successful cereal manufacturing business that began in a small factory at 213 Cedar Avenue. In 1923, Arthur McCallum became president of the Flako Products Corporation and his wife, *Daily Home News* reporter Helen G. McCallum, became secretary-treasurer. They moved their operations to bigger quarters at 314 Cleveland Avenue and offered many Highland Park residents employment through the decade of the Depression. (Highland Park Historical Society.)

50

Four

A RARITAN
AVENUE ADDRESS

A VIEW FROM THE BRIDGE, C. 1937. The old cobblestones and abandoned trolley tracks on the Albany Street Bridge continue up Raritan Avenue's hill in this early morning view. The "L" on the circular signpost to the right is a Lincoln Highway marker. In 1937, the hilltop house at 39 Raritan Avenue was home to Maud and Milton Swartsbaugh. (Borough of Highland Park Historical Commission.)

No. 66 Raritan Avenue, 1908. Hoagland's Highland Park Pharmacy was located on the corner of Raritan and Cedar Avenues. Arthur Wykoff and Joseph Barlow ran the suburban branch of this New Brunswick business. As an integral center for social gatherings, the drug store held the first post office and soda fountain. The old Bissett House across the street is reflected in the front window. Joe Barlow worked here until he opened his own store further up Raritan Avenue in 1917. (Juanita Barlow Messer.)

The Raritan Avenue Business Section, c. 1910. This postcard shows Highland Park's downtown at the beginning of the 20th century on Raritan Avenue's south side, between First and Cedar Avenues. (Carolyn Kuhlthau.)

NO. 78 RARITAN AVENUE, 1891. An ad from the 1891 New Brunswick Directory (above) announces the presence of Anthony J. Gebhardt's "Choice Family Groceries" on Raritan Avenue at the corner of South First Avenue. Established in 1889 as Highland Park's first general store, it was the sole source for groceries for four years. By 1908, Gebhardt boasted of having three delivery wagons, six employees, and a telephone. His building became known as Gebhardt's Corner and it was the starting and ending point for round-trip bicycle races to Metuchen. Gebhardt served on the first borough council as tax collector, a position that remained in the family, for his nephew, "Uncle Ben" Gebhardt, later held the same job for 40 years. The three-story building stood until the 1960s, when its upper stories were dismantled. Now the first floor houses the Park Deli. The drawing below is another from the border of businesses on the 1910 Aero-View Map of New Brunswick. (Library of Congress Geography and Maps Division.)

A. J. GEBHARDT, GROCERIES & PROVISIONS.

No. 125 Raritan Avenue, c. 1915. Vreeland & Herbert had a real estate and insurance business at this modest one-story office building on Raritan Avenue. Run by Minedert Vreeland and fire department treasurer Edwin W. Herbert, the business was in operation between 1913 and 1921. The building was replaced by Anton Sprincel's tailor shop. (Edith Lenetti.)

No. 125 Raritan Avenue, c. 1946. As a youth, John Lenetti apprenticed to tailor Anton Sprincel and worked for him for many years. He took over the business in 1946 and proudly stands in his Oxford bags at the doorway of his new tailor shop. The pile of clothes in the window is ready to be cleaned. The Robert Thomas Bicycle Shop also shared this building. (Edith Lenetti.)

No. 127 Raritan Avenue, 1920. With its prime downtown location and its showroom for luxury car sales, Sexton's Garage reached the pinnacle of Highland Park's growing automobile business. Joining several service garages and used car dealers, Sexton's sold brand new Essex and Hudson automobiles. Speedsters cost $1,645 and sedans were $2,295 (freight and tax extra). Competition came when George H. Gilbert opened his Chrysler sales office across the street at 114 Raritan Avenue in the late 1920s, as seen below in an advertisement from the Baptist Church's 1929 publication, *The Complete Hostess*. (Juanita Barlow Messer.)

DE SOTO SIX-SEDAN

DE SOTO SIX

CHRYSLER MOTORS PRODUCT

G. H. GILBERT

114 Raritan Avenue, Highland Park

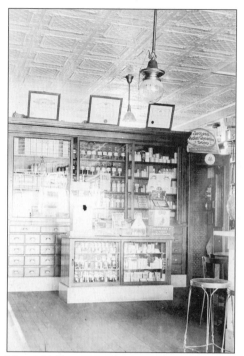

NO. 128 RARITAN AVENUE, INSIDE AND OUT, 1918. Joseph H. Barlow, a former manager of Hoagland's Highland Park Pharmacy, opened his own business on March 17, 1917. "Doc" Barlow dispensed more than pills and medical advice. His milk shakes and sodas were a hit on warm summer evenings. He also sold tickets for Rutgers football games, World War I stamps, war bonds, and Kodak cameras. He was a good amateur photographer and this book contains many images he took that his daughter fortuitously saved. This building now holds Chapter One Cafe and Books and its pressed tin ceiling remains intact. (Juanita Barlow Messer.)

NO. 137 RARITAN AVENUE, 1920. This old jitney bus picked the best spot to lose its tire, right in front of William, Fannie and Goldie Himelstein's confectionery! Next door, the firehouse stands with its tall bell tower at 141 Raritan Avenue. From 1905 to 1920, the firehouse also housed the justice of the peace, the police department, and the borough council meeting room upstairs. (Juanita Barlow Messer.)

No. 212 Raritan Avenue, 1892 (above) and 1894 (below). The seasons come and go and little children grow fastest. Not all the buildings along Raritan Avenue held businesses. For many years, families have lived in homes along the main street. The Malmros family homestead (# 30, 1888 map) is pictured here two years and two seasons apart. In the top photo, Gustava Malmros holds one-year-old Walter while five-year-old Elizabeth stands next to her. In the bottom photograph, taken two years later, the children sit on the steps in the summertime. (Douglas Eden.)

No. 243 Raritan Avenue, c. 1921. Gustaf Yourstone on the left and George Yourstone on the right ran their butcher shop on Raritan Avenue in the early 1920s. The name of the man in the middle is not known. In a *Daily Home News* "Highland Park Notes" article in February 1923, their tasteful display of lamb caught the eye of a local reporter, who also mentioned that veal would be on view the following week. A short-lived venture here, the butcher shop was taken over by the Eden family in the mid-1920s and the Yourstones opened a shop in nearby Metuchen. (Enid Yourstone.)

No. 248 Raritan Avenue, c. 1944. Victor Fais owned and operated the Third Avenue Sweet Shop from 1932 to 1979 and is partly responsible for the town's well-founded notion that there used to be a sweet shop on every corner. He also would come to own the Fifth Avenue Sweet Shop. (Rebecca Globus.)

The Third Avenue Sweet Shop, c. 1944. "These boys played the pinball machine endlessly," stated Florence Fais when looking at the 1944 snapshot taken in her father's Third Avenue Sweet Shop. The building is still owned by the Fais family, although the business was renamed the Corner Confectionery by the Williams family in 1979. (Rebecca Globus.)

Sally's Tavern-Restaurant Air Conditioned. Main Dining Room. 247 Raritan Ave. Highland Park, N.J. N.B. 2-7718

No. 247 Raritan Avenue, c. 1948. Sarah (nicknamed Sally) and David Tishler started a tavern on the corner of Raritan and North Third Avenues in the mid-1930s. During the war years, Sally served food out of a small kitchen, and in 1948 the large dining room pictured in the above postcard was added on to the back of the tavern along N. Third Avenue. Keeping the business in the family, Sally's daughter Dorothy and Dorothy's husband, Jerry Miller, bought the restaurant in 1952. The house next door at 245 Raritan was incorporated into the original structure during the early 1950s and helped promote Sally's in becoming Highland Park's finest dining establishment. Murals painted by Bruce McPhail and George Brecht in 1954 graced the main dining room walls and were duplicated on printed placemats (below). (Lilian Handel and Susan Marchand.)

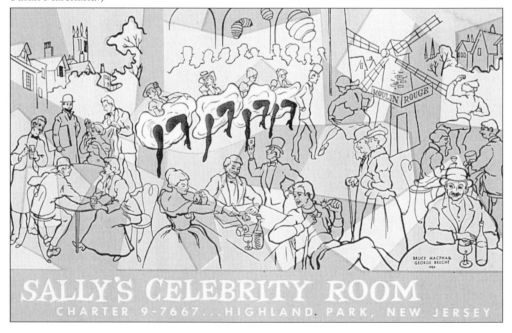

SALLY'S CELEBRITY ROOM
CHARTER 9-7667...HIGHLAND PARK, NEW JERSEY

THE 300 BLOCK OF RARITAN AVENUE, C. 1960. Taking advantage of no traffic on this usually busy avenue, Joseph Koye captured a winter wonderland view of Raritan's 300 block between Third and Fourth Avenues one early December morning. While some of the businesses seen here no longer exist, others have taken their places along Highland Park's thriving main street. (Rich Odato.)

NO. 314 RARITAN AVENUE, C. 1935. Ah, the smell inside a bakery can not be beat on a cold winter day. Helen Engelhardt Arky and Moe Engelhardt wait on customers from behind the cake counter at the Highland Park Bakery. Rose and David Engelhardt owned this store from 1924 to 1940. With generous hearts, they helped many customers through the economic slump of the years of the Great Depression. (Harriet Tabak.)

THE STEIN BUILDING, C. 1966. This is one photograph from a series Joseph Koye made documenting the condition of Raritan Avenue businesses in the 1960s. The Stein Building, built in 1925 at the corner of Raritan and North Fourth Avenues, has housed the Presto Restaurant, Penny's, the Park Sweet Shop, and Pino's Market, among many others. (Highland Park Historical Society.)

NO. 402 RARITAN AVENUE, 1955. With a vantage point from the roof of the Stein Building, Dr. Sydney F. Smith's house, catty-corner across the street, lends itself beautifully as a backdrop for the Highland Park 50th Anniversary Parade. High school baton twirlers led the Highland Park Fire Department in this 1955 celebration. (Highland Park Historical Society.)

No. 401–411 Raritan Avenue, 1922. This billboard promises a building that would become the center of community life in Highland Park. Located on the corner of Raritan and North Fourth Avenues, the Masonic Lodge has been home to municipal offices, the post office, the public library, religious congregations, and almost every kind of business in town during its long life. (Juanita Barlow Messer.)

Laying the Cornerstone, 1922. The first spadeful of dirt was turned for the Masonic Lodge on November 24, 1922, by Mayor Robert Wood Johnson Jr. The cornerstone was laid on December 16, 1922, accompanied by appropriate Masonic ceremonies. Participants wore small lapel buttons commemorating the occasion. Constructed by members of the Masonic Order, the building cost over $225,000. (Douglas Eden.)

No. 401 Raritan Avenue, 1923. Relocating uptown to the corner store in August of 1923, Barlow's Drug Store was the first business to move into the new Masonic Lodge. With more space and a dark wood interior, the new store created a posh atmosphere for customers. While stores were located on the front first floor, the second story held offices. The back section, covered in diamond pattern brickwork, was three stories tall and held a large auditorium that was among the area's grandest. It housed a roller skating academy, dance marathons, basketball games, boxing and wrestling matches, and concerts. Notable conductors included Ozzie Nelson and the town's own Connie Atkinson Jr., who led his Berkely-Carteret Band in many performances. (Juanita Barlow Messer.)

The Masonic Temple, c. 1959. The stores on the street level reflect the changing face of commerce in this 1959 snapshot. Bingo games became very popular during this era. The Masonic Building also received a new neighbor by this time, the Acme supermarket. (Borough of Highland Park Historical Commission.)

No. 415 Raritan Avenue, c. 1966. This view, another from Joseph Koye's series, shows the Metropolitan Life Insurance Building, which replaced the Acme Food Market. In 1974, the New Brunswick congregation Ohav Emeth purchased the building and it soon became Highland Park's third synagogue. (Highland Park Historical Society.)

The 500 Block of Raritan Avenue, 1940. A Public Service bus on line 134 between Newark and New Brunswick was photographed on July 8, 1940, as it passed in front of the Ausonia Apartments and several 1920s commercial buildings on Raritan Avenue's north side between Fifth and Sixth Avenues. (Bill Christian.)

A VIEW FROM THE HIGHLAND PARK HOTEL, 1948. The double-feature movies listed on the theater's marquee to the left are two 1948 releases, *That Wonderful Urge* and *Belle Star's Daughter*. Once the Block Park Theater, it changed hands in 1943 to become the RKO Reade. The diagonal road on the right is Raritan Avenue, Highland Park's main street. (Felix Farenga.)

Five

"PEOPLE MOVE HERE FOR THE SCHOOLS"

A Dark Day for a Picture, c. 1886. Set up against the brick wall of the first schoolhouse, the children in one of Miss Chrissie Bartle's earliest classes hold themselves steady. Miss Bartle sits on the right and Helen Kitchenmeister, the florist's daughter, is second to the left in the front row. In the third row, Frank Atkinson is third to the left of Miss Bartle. (The Atkinson Family.)

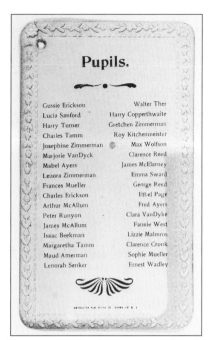

Souvenir

Highland Park School

DISTRICT NO. 2.
GRAMMAR DEPARTMENT.

Raritan Township,
Middlesex Co., N. J.

1899

PRESENTED BY

Thos. G. Van Kirk,
TEACHER.

SCHOOL BOARD

Edward B. Dana, M. D. - President
R. Bruce Crowell, D. C.
William E. Burns   William T. Werner
George W. Bissett   Edward J. Drake
William Garman   George W. Mead
W. A. Spencer

Pupils.

Gussie Erickson	Walter Ther
Lucia Sanford	Harry Copperthwaite
Harry Turner	Gretchen Zimmerman
Charles Tamm	Roy Kitchenmeister
Josephine Zimmerman	Max Wolfson
Marjorie VanDyck	Clarence Reed
Mabel Ayers	James McElarney
Lenora Zimmerman	Emma Sward
Frances Mueller	George Reed
Charles Erickson	Ethel Page
Arthur McAllum	Fred Ayers
Peter Runyon	Clara VanDyke
James McAllum	Fannie West
Isaac Beekman	Lizzie Malmros
Margaretha Tamm	Clarence Cronk
Maud Amerman	Sophie Mueller
Lenorah Senker	Ernest Wadley

A SCHOOL SOUVENIR, 1899. In reading the list of student names, familiar ones are found, although some are misspelled. Mabel and Fred Ayers (Ayres) are related to the milkman and we have seen Lizzie (Elizabeth) Malmros on her front steps at 212 Raritan Avenue. Arthur McAllum (McCallum) would later become an important local businessman in the 1930s as owner of the Flako Company, and Harry Turner was the oldest son of Turner Tubes owner John S. Turner. Roy Kitchenmeister is the florist's child. (Douglas Eden.)

HIGHLAND PARK SCHOOL, C. 1910. The school population expanded rapidly, and by 1906 the three-room school became inadequate. The original one-room school built in 1886 was sold at auction to the Highland Park Reformed Church for $37 and moved to their grounds. The school kept the 1890 and 1897 one-room additions; the four-room brick building in this postcard view was built in front of them. Designed in the Colonial Revival style by Alexander Merchant, Highland Park now had a six-room schoolhouse. (Borough of Highland Park Historical Commission.)

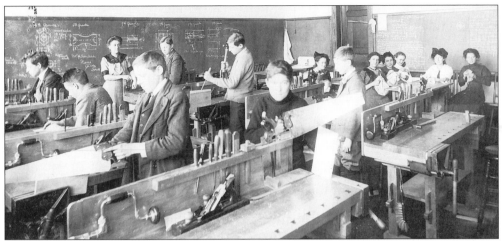

MORE THAN THE THREE R'S, 1913. Manual training teacher Rosena C. Foster conducts a segregated class of woodworking and sewing at the Highland Park School. While the girls attended to their needlework, the boys had tool time. By the early teens, the school population had grown to an extent where special classes could be offered. In 1910, Leo Mullen was hired to teach music. In 1911, the first manual training schedule was sent to the state department for approval. A drawing class started in 1914. (Borough of Highland Park Historical Commission.)

LAFAYETTE'S FOURTH GRADERS, 1918. During the 1918–19 school year, Elizabeth Connor's fourth grade class experienced two major historical events—they observed the Armistice of November 11, 1918, which ended the War to End All Wars, and they lived through the "Spanish" influenza epidemic, which temporarily forbade public assembly, including school. In the autumn of 1918, 18,306 people died in New Jersey, and the department of health tallied 211,410 cases of flu and pneumonia throughout the state. (Juanita Barlow Messer.)

A New Wing, A New Name, 1938. By 1910, the six room school was overflowing with children and more classrooms were needed. The two old classrooms in the rear were demolished and a brick two-story, six-room addition enlarged the Highland Park school to ten rooms. On April 14, 1915, the school's name became Lafayette. Two years later, this four-room wing, designed by Alexander Merchant, was built along South Second Avenue. After receiving several more additions throughout the years, in 1983 Lafayette was sold and converted into condominiums. (Bernice Bernstein Archive, Highland Park Historical Society.)

Jackets and Skirts, 1919. These Lafayette School fifth grade students strike a classic pose dressed in their best jackets and skirts. The rigidity of the desks and the starkness of the classroom with walls of blackboards are a far cry from today's colorful classroom environments. The iron-clad desks seen in numerous old school photographs held inkwells filled with black liquid for fountain pens. (Juanita Barlow Messer.)

MAY DAY, 1922. The maypole may be missing, but this is certainly a celebration of the coming of spring. These young ladies, dressed all in white and trailing streamers, demonstrate both grace and coordination in Lafayette School's seasonal program. The celebrations were held throughout the United States on the first day of every May. The teacher on the right is Meryl Deinzer, Lafayette's physical education teacher. (Juanita Barlow Messer.)

FOLK DANCING, 1933. First graders performed *The Sleeping Princess.* Sixth grade boys ran relay races. Dressed in colorful and authentic costumes, Lafayette's pupils presented an exhibit of songs and dances from around the world. The May Fourth event, co-sponsored by the PTA and school authorities, was part of the regular school program and the result of several months' work. Proceeds from the admission fee of 10¢ went toward the purchase of playground equipment. (Bernice Bernstein Archive, Highland Park Historical Society.)

IRVING'S BOYS OF SUMMER, 1933. There were many vacant lots in Highland Park and baseball was a popular sport among children of all ages. Here, Irving School's team displays the trophy it won by defeating both Lafayette and Hamilton Schools in the summer championship. From left to right are as follows: (kneeling) Art Sinibaldi, August Muscle, Joe Policastro, Renzo Odato and Rick Pisciotta; (standing) Buddy Haskins, Willmore Henry, and Walter Haskins. (Richard Pisciotta.)

THIRD GRADE, IRVING SCHOOL, 1918. These children should be smiling! They have a new four-room brick schoolhouse. From October 22, 1913, until January 1916, the children of the Race Track district had attended the Annex School at rented rooms in the Middlesex Bowling Club at 73 Woodbridge Avenue. That building no longer exists. Daniel A. Rutolo, sixth from the right in the front row, found his old school picture and contributed it to the New Brunswick Free Public Library. The teacher is unidentified, but may be Miss Babbage.

ARCHITECTURAL TWINS, C. 1940S. After enrollment reached 458 children, the concept of neighborhood schools came to fruition in town-wide discussions during 1914. A plan calling for two separate neighborhood schools was chosen in a vote and Alexander Merchant drew up one set of plans for the two structures. Hamilton School on North Third Avenue was finished first and opened on November 22, 1915. Irving School on Central and South Eleventh Avenues opened two months later on January 8, 1916. Both schools received four-room additions finished in 1921. In the photograph above, Irving School proudly shows off its solid construction. Seen in the PTA photograph below, Hamilton was covered in ivy by the 1940s. Although they were identical architecturally, these schools served very diverse populations. Irving educated the children of recent immigrants largely of the working class while Hamilton served the children of Highland Park's middle and upper classes from Livingston Manor and other north side houses. (Gerard T. Schultz and Bernice Bernstein Archive, Highland Park Historical Society.)

THE HAMILTON HIGHLIGHTS STAFF, 1940. Standing by their press, the staff of the *Hamilton Highlights* included, from left to right, James Schuyler, Jane Woodruff, Martin Spritzer, Alvin Rodoff, Mary Alice Sherman, Gutrich Briethoff, and Terry Gopin. (Borough of Highland Park Historical Commission.)

THE STRAWBERRY FESTIVAL AT HAMILTON, 1941. Strawberry festivals took place in the first half of the 20th century and were considered great fund-raisers. At their June 2 get-together, these Hamilton School socialites waited for the festivities to begin. (Borough of Highland Park Historical Commission.)

FRANKLIN JUNIOR HIGH SCHOOL, 1940. Demand for a junior high school began as early as 1918. However, it was not until 1924, after several sites were considered, that the Solomon-Maher Tract, 7 acres of land on Montgomery Street and North Fifth Avenue, was purchased for $37,000. Alexander Merchant submitted plans for the new Georgian Revival-style building. A $280,912 contract went to the Nora & Nora Construction Company. Opened in September of 1926, a formal dedication ceremony took place on October 14 that included the American Legion's placement of a donated cannon on the new school's front yard, seen in the picture postcard below. The name Franklin Junior High School was chosen one month after the dedication. This school served children only up to the tenth grade. Highland Parkites continued finishing high school at either New Brunswick High or Metuchen High School until 1937, when our senior high school was established. (Bernice Bernstein Archive, Highland Park Historical Society and Eleanor Williams.)

THE TEAM WARMS UP, 1938. A full sports program resulted from the creation of the senior high school in 1937. A young football team is shown here stretching before a game. The early years were difficult, but by 1942 the Highland Park Owls were conference champions. A winning tradition was established under the leadership of Bus Lepine and Jay Dakelman. Today, alumnus Joe Policastro, Highland Park's all-state quarterback, continues the work of his former coaches. (Bernice Bernstein Archive, Highland Park Historical Society.)

FROM DINKS TO SADDLE SHOES, 1938. Highland Park's first group of high school cheerleaders sure look swell from head to toe in their new uniforms. From left to right they are coach Lee Hoagland, Clare Strapp, Annette De Blon, captain Ann Gray, Margaret Bishop, and Nina Vincent. (Bernice Bernstein Archive, Highland Park Historical Society.)

THE MASCOT'S LETTER SWEATER, 1938.
"Spike," the high school mascot, and his
friend, Ed Garretson, cheered for the home
team. Today, the wise owl is the high
school's mascot. (Bernice Bernstein
Archive, Highland Park Historical Society.)

STRIKE UP THE BAND, C. 1943. A few years after becoming a senior high school, Highland
Park had a 45-piece uniformed band under the direction of Condit Atkinson Jr. In 1955, his
son, Condit Atkinson III, took over the position of music director. In this 1943 group portrait,
father stands on the left next to his son, who is wrapped up in a sousaphone. (The Atkinson
Family.)

OVERCROWDED SCHOOLS, 1965. The post-World War II baby boom and the construction of large apartment complexes in the late 1950s resulted in dramatic overcrowding. By the 1960s, classes were being conducted in hallways, broom closets, and even in one school's boiler room. Classrooms had to be rented from the Reformed Church. These boys, changing for gym class in Irving School's basement hallway, were photographed by Joseph Koye, part of a series that documented the lack of facilities. (John Powell.)

HONORING MISS CHRISSIE BARTLE, 1967. Bartle School, named for Highland Park's first public schoolteacher and designed by the architectural firm Eckert and Gatarz, opened in 1967 on a 4.2-acre plot at South Fifth and Mansfield Avenues. It originally housed middle school grades six, seven, and eight. With many changes since 1967, Highland Park's 1,400 public school students are currently consolidated at Irving School (K–2), Bartle (3–6), the new middle school (7–8) next to the high school, and the high school (9–12). In the 1980s, Hamilton became a private school and Lafayette was transformed into condominiums. (Borough of Highland Park Historical Commission.)

ST. PAUL'S SCHOOL, 1950. A decision made on April 5, 1926, led to the construction of the parochial school and auditorium next to St. Paul's Church at 502 Raritan Avenue. General contractor John L. Snitzler of New Brunswick built the building, designed by Perth Amboy architect George W. Brooks, for $130,000. After the formal cornerstone laying and dedication on June 26, 1927, the school opened two months later on September 12 to 80 pupils in the first five grades. Teachers from the Third Order of Fransiscan Sisters were led by principal Mother Mary Isabella. The school continued to grow, with the highest enrollment coming in 1952. During the 1980s, a slow decline in enrollment eventually led to the school's closure on June 11, 1992. (Church of Saint Paul the Apostle.)

EIGHTH GRADE CLASS PICTURE, 1952. Standing on the front steps of the church of St. Paul, these 33 students graduated during the peak years of St. Paul's School. (Gerard T. Schultz.)

79

THE HEBREW SCHOOL, 1930. Rabbi Isadore Shalom Ravetch quizzed his pupils on Jewish history in the newly constructed Highland Park Conservative Temple at 109 North Third Avenue. Grace Winfield, standing in the back, was assistant teacher. The idea for a Hebrew school in Highland Park began in 1926, when a group of men returning from Rosh Hoshanah services in New Brunswick decided their children should not have to travel across the river for religious instruction. They pledged $5,000 to establish a Talmud Torah. A vacant store was rented on North Fourth Avenue and Rabbi I. Horowitz was engaged to teach. On April 26, 1930, the Highland Park Hebrew School Association received its charter from the state of New Jersey. By June of 1930, the Highland Park Conservative Temple on North Third Avenue near Montgomery Street was completed. Rabbi Ravetch was the spiritual leader who organized four daily after-school classes. The children, ranging in age from 7 to 15, continued receiving instruction in Hebrew and the bible while adding Hebrew literature and Jewish history. This small building, with a 1961 addition on its facade, is now the Masonic Lodge. (Highland Park Conservative Temple.)

Six

SERVICE TO THE
COMMUNITY AND
COUNTRY

IN FULL DRESS, 1917. They may have hung the flag incorrectly, but they look patriotic anyway! The Highland Park Volunteer Fire Department assembled in front of the old firehouse on Raritan Avenue. Their first full dress uniforms resemble those of the Civil War. Thanks, fire fighters, for over 100 years of service to the community. (Ex-Fire Chief John Robert Toth.)

OUT OF UNIFORM, 1922. Gerald Hussey dressed as a clown for the fire department's group portrait showing off their new dress uniforms, which were worn in parades. The photograph was taken by Carl C. Francis in front of the firehouse at 141 Raritan Avenue. In the 1920s, a local

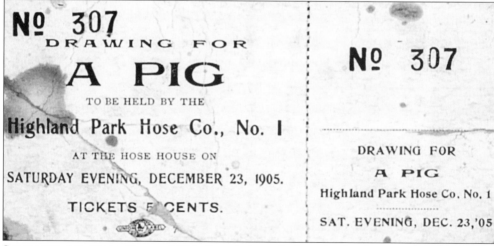

SAVED FOR ALL THESE YEARS, 1905. Even in its early days, the fire department held raffles as fund-raisers. Throughout the years, it has been involved in numerous social service projects, including aiding the needy, throwing Christmas parties for borough children, and making donations to the high school's athletic and music departments, as well as to the Highland Park Historical Society. (Juanita Barlow Messer.)

newspaper reported that the department ranked among "the best of the volunteer departments in the State of New Jersey." (Highland Park Volunteer Fire Department.)

A FIREMAN'S RESCUE, 1987. Sitting next to John Donnelly, ex-chief Gerard T. Schultz drives his pride and joy, an old La France pumper, past the Brody House, which once existed at 47 Raritan Avenue. The truck cost $11,500 in 1920 and is believed to be the second motorized apparatus purchased by the fire department. Considered the finest engine of its day, by 1961 the borough sold it at auction for $100. Schultz traced its whereabouts from a junkyard to an auto dealer and ultimately to the private collector who parted with it. Returning to Highland Park in excellent condition in 1982, it is now used for parades, such as this one on Memorial Day. (Ex-Fire Chief Gerard T. Schultz.)

THE AMERICAN LA FRANCE, 1922. After a contentious two-year period between authorization for funds and its actual purchase, the fire department finally received their American La France fire truck in 1915. A bond issue raised funds for the $5,000 needed to purchase it and a town-wide fire alarm system. Proudly standing by the apparatus are William D. Stelle, Assistant Chief Harry R. Singer, Ross Reed, and future mayor Cornelius B. McCrelis. Charles Malmros Jr. sits at the wheel. (Ex-Fire Chief Gerard T. Schultz.)

A QUAD PUMPER LADDER TRUCK, 1949. Photographed in Donaldson Park, this 1928 White fire engine had superior cargo capacity for extra hose, pumps, and ground ladders with 50-foot extensions. Purchased to keep pace with the rapid growth of residential properties, the fire truck could pump water faster and farther than the two La France engines. Search lights helped illuminate the scenes of nighttime fires. (Highland Park Volunteer Fire Department.)

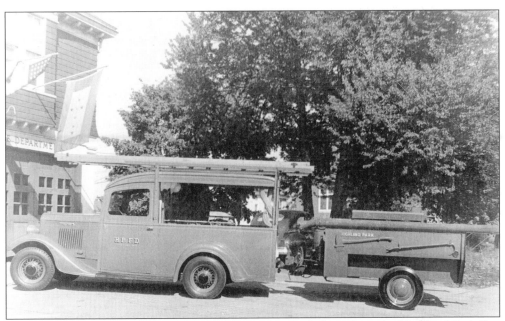

AN AUXILIARY TRUCK AND TRAILER, 1942. For general alarm fires, the Highland Park Fire Auxiliary would be called into action. This reserve force of assistants purchased a truck and trailer to haul extra hose, ladders, portable pumps, and barriers to fire scenes. The group was very active during the 1940s and 1950s. (Highland Park Volunteer Fire Department.)

GOLDEN JUBILEE, 1949. Highland Park's firehouse is adorned with bunting to celebrate the 50th anniversary of the creation of the Highland Park Hose Company. (The fire department was formed in 1913.) Built in 1904 on land owned by the hose company, in 1922 this unpretentious structure on Raritan Avenue near Second Avenue was hailed as "the one place of real importance in this community." The lower floor housed motor equipment, and the upper floor was used for meetings. The original building, enlarged several times, served as headquarters until 1955, when the department moved to its present location at 222 South Fifth Avenue. The 95-year-old building now houses a dry cleaner. (Highland Park Volunteer Fire Department.)

LIFE IMITATES ART, 1927. The fire department sponsored dances, entertainment, and other frolics that were always enjoyable and profitable. Six hundred rang in 1928 at the annual New Year's Eve party in the Masonic auditorium. Radio artists provided by the Sykes Entertainment Bureau included a banjo and accordion act, a magician, and a minstrel show. No one realized that the program cover's drawing, which bore an uncanny resemblance to the Masonic Building, presaged an event 37 years later. (Highland Park Historical Society.)

NO BINGO THIS WEEK, 1965. In an ironic twist of fate, bingo games sponsored by the fire department became homeless when, on March 10, 1965, the Masonic Temple was nearly destroyed in a double general alarm fire. Starting in a maintenance room on the second floor, the fire spread through a false ceiling and engulfed the upper floor. A concrete floor prevented its spread to the bottom floor. With its upper story gone, the structure remains as a one-story commercial building. Charring is visible along the top course of its North Fourth Avenue side. (Ex-Fire Chief John Robert Toth.)

HIGHLAND PARK'S FINEST, 1939. Highland Park's first law officer was Fielding Lucas, who served as a marshal until 1923. George C. Bedford became the first full-time uniformed policeman in 1911. By 1924, there were six marshals, who were then organized into a regular police department in 1926. By 1939, the force had grown to 11 men. Pictured here are, from left to right, Bob Vanderhof, John Sorensen, Stephen Jacobs, LeRoy Fuller, Lieutenant Fred Schedig, Chief Alfred Smalley, Lieutenant Frederick Woerner, Ira Lee Messer, Harry Purcell, Andrew Schritenthal, and Robert Eadie. (Juanita Barlow Messer.)

GOLDEN JUBILEE PARADE, 1955. The few members of the police department who were not directing traffic and controlling the crowds could actually be participants in the Highland Park 50th Anniversary Parade. By 1955, the squad had grown significantly, having over 90 reserves. (Borough of Highland Park Historical Commission.)

THE WAR TO END ALL WARS, 1917. Residents lined up to see the calvary led by John J. Pershing make its way to Camp Raritan. Soon after the declaration of war on April 6, 1917, President Wilson signed the draft act and the duties of war usurped the vocations of peace. Streets everywhere were filled with marching troops. Over 45 young men from Highland Park were called for active duty. Mayor Russell E. Watson and the Home Defense League raised funds and increased patriotic work. Camp Raritan was established nearby and became one of the most important supply depots in the United States. On Armistice Day, November 11, 1918, there were 6,325 men in the camp. These snapshots were taken looking northwest from 128 Raritan Avenue and show the wooded north side between Adelaide and Second Avenues. (Juanita Barlow Messer.)

DOUGHBOY STATUE UNVEILING, 1921. In these two photographs by Carl C. Francis, taken moments apart, the granite World War I "Doughboy" statue at the intersection of Woodbridge and Raritan Avenue is revealed before a gathering of 2,000 onlookers. By November, in a fund-raising effort that began in March, $4,000 had been raised in door-to-door canvasses. Donors were listed in the *Highland Park Press*. A newspaper account states that at the November 11 ceremony, speeches and a memorial poem followed two minutes of silence at noon. Written by William J. Fitzgerald, Professor E. Livingston Barbour read this work, which began, "Tread softly, friend, and bow the head in memory of our honored dead . . ." When finished, the 48-star flag was removed by four servicemen to the reports of a three-gun salute. Marguerite and Kathleen Wheatley laid a wreath at the monument's base in honor of veterans from both the Spanish-American War and the Great War. Patriotic songs and Highland Park's biggest parade followed the unveiling and the day's festivities ended with an invitational dance sponsored by the American Legion. (Juanita Barlow Messer.)

AMERICAN LEGION DRUM AND BUGLE CORPS, 1932. These sharp uniforms of French blue cloth, block leather puttees, Sam Brown belts, and helmets arrived just in time for the 1929 Memorial Day Parade. A very active and civic-minded organization, Highland Park Post 88 sponsored its own Boy Scout troop, organized Community Night to encourage cooperative neighborhood spirit, held Christmas Eve celebrations at the Soldiers Monument, and made donations such as the Franklin Junior High School's cannon. Post 88 received its charter on July 25, 1921, making it the 13th such post in Middlesex County. John Hunter was the first post commander and meetings were held in rooms over Hodges' Garage on North Second Avenue. In 1931, the post received title to 127 Benner Street, which served as its headquarters until it was sold in 1949. The post now has a modest building at 808 Raritan Avenue. (American Legion Post 88.)

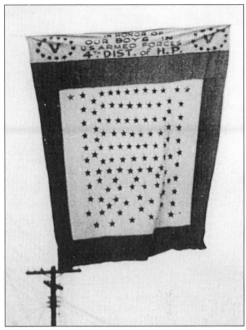

STARS AND STRIPES, C. 1943. Mrs. Cornelia Peters's service flag with stars for individual Highland Park men and women in the Armed Services hangs suspended over Magnolia Street near her South Seventh Avenue home. In less than 25 years, the United States was involved in another major world struggle, despite President Franklin Delano Roosevelt's statement, "I have seen war . . . and I hate war." Patriotism permeated the town. With a population of 9,000, more than 1,000 were in the Armed Forces. In addition to service flags, an honor roll bearing the names of those who were in the war was erected on South Fourth Avenue. (Frances Pieters.)

ON THE HOME FRONT, C. 1943. Air raid warden Eleanor Burns starts her victory garden, one of many in town. While Highland Park residents contributed to the war efforts, developments outside were affecting our population. The nearby Raritan Arsenal supplied weapons, parts, and vehicles to East Coast ports. Camp Kilmer was established and nearly five million soldiers passed through there, either to or from the European Theater. By 1943, there were eight U.S.O. sites in the immediate area. (Pat Burns Toth.)

Our Own Post Office Branch, 1937. In 1891, the Postal Service offered three deliveries a day and post boxes were at every corner. Limited mailing services were available at the Highland Park Pharmacy from 1908 until 1919, then at Gebhardt's Grocery. On December 1, 1926, a small branch office of the U.S. Postal Service opened in the Masonic Building at 11 North Fourth Avenue. This allowed Superintendent James Quakenboss, in charge of three carriers, to have an office fully equipped to handle all postal business. The workstation was photographed in 1937. (Alexander Library Special Collections and University Archives.)

A Field Trip to the Post Office, 1953. The post office moved from the Masonic Building to what is now the Pomerantz Building at 300 Raritan Avenue in 1940. In 1949 it relocated to this one-story building at 17 North Fourth Avenue. These Irving School second graders had a tour four years later. Now painted white, this building houses the Dance Exchange. The post office moved once again in the 1960s to Raritan Avenue. (Joanne Pisciotta.)

PTA Class Mothers, Lafayette, 1938. Middlesex County's first parents and teachers group, the School Auxiliary, was organized in Highland Park in 1905. With merely a name change in 1912, the Parent-Teacher Association (PTA) continued its predecessor's advocacy for children's education. Promoting good communications between school, home, and community, this group also participated in the state organization whose annual conventions presented tough political issues resulting in numerous legislative actions. This 1938 photograph was included in Lafayette School's PTA publicity book produced as required for membership in the state organization. (Bernice Bernstein Archive, Highland Park Historical Society.)

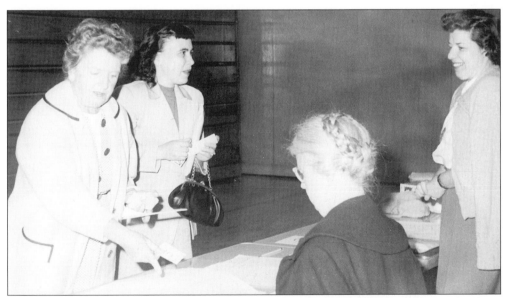

Democracy in Action, 1961. Continuing the tradition of promoting good citizenship born in 1920, members of the non-partisan League of Women Voters helped conduct polling on Survey Day in 1961. Elizabeth Cottle and Sally Shure assist Grace Hopkins and Pat Zawadsky. Highland Park's branch began in 1936 with meetings at Mrs. Marshall's 15 North Seventh Avenue home. Along with staffing elections, these activists wrote informational town guides and sponsored candidate debates. (Borough of Highland Park Historical Commission.)

A Borough Council Meeting, 1923. Joseph De Maria was another active photographer in the 1920s. Here he has posed the 1923 Borough Council around the table in chambers, most likely at their new offices in the Masonic Building. From 1905 to 1923, the council held their official business meetings at the firehouse and at Hodges' Garage. Needing more spacious quarters, the borough eventually rented upper floor rooms at the Masonic Building. (Douglas Eden.)

A Borough Hall of Our Own, 1951. Taking over the old Barnwell House at 11 South Fourth Avenue, Borough Hall finally had a place of its own. With a population nearing 10,000 residents, the services offered by official departments and elected officials exceeded the space at the Masonic. Of course, the borough eventually outgrew this building, and in 1979 the municipal offices were relocated to 221 South Fifth Avenue. (Will Gainfort Collection, Alexander Library Special Collections.)

THE WPA SCULPTS A POND, 1939. The Great Depression in the 1930s and Roosevelt's New Deal fashioned the largest public works program in the history of the United States. Works Progress Administration (WPA) jobs in Highland Park included street cleaning, shade tree trimming, janitorial services for the schools, and the construction Johnson Park. A WPA photographer standing on the railroad embankment took this view of the pond, just to the north, between River Road and the Raritan River. Today, this earthwork can be seen safely through train windows. (National Archives and Records Administration.)

THE PUBLIC WORKS DEPARTMENT, 1959. Winning the Engineers of America award in 1930 as the most beautiful engineering structure of the year, Morris Goodkind's Route 1 Bridge creates a dramatic backdrop as a public works employee maneuvers the dirt of Highland Park's landfill. Covering an area that used to be called the Meadows, the landfill had a short life span and was closed in the 1960s. (Pat Burns Toth.)

FIRST CAME AN AMBULANCE, 1949. When Highland Park was given an ambulance in 1949 there was only one other in the area. Owned by the New Brunswick Fire Department, it served over 50,000 people. Highland Park's first ambulance, a fully equipped 1949 Meteor Cadillac, was donated by Helen G. and Arthur McCallum through their Flako Products Corporation. The ambulance was housed, rent free, at the MacKinney Oil Building until a headquarters could be completed. The First Aid Squad got its start in 1949 after Ferdinand Denhard and others took first aid classes from the Milltown Rescue Squad. (Highland Park First Aid Squad.)

PUBLIC SUPPORT, 1951. In April 1950, Mayor Alvah H. Cole urged town-wide support for a campaign to raise $12,000 to start building new headquarters for the First Aid Squad. The borough donated land on South Eleventh Avenue and Arcadia Street. The next year, parades, door-to-door solicitations, and neighborhood contests were conducted to raise additional funds to complete the building and pay for operating costs. Organizers, including the McCallums, posed for this publicity shot. (Will Gainfort Collection, Alexander Library Special Collections.)

AT LAST, A HEADQUARTERS, 1952. Construction of the First Aid Squad Building began on June 1, 1950. It was truly a public affair, with local companies donating material and labor. On Saturday, June 14, 1952, following a gala parade, the building was formally dedicated by Mayor DeCoster. Arcadia Street was renamed McCallum in honor of the donors who helped make the vision of a First Aid Squad a reality. An addition to the building was made in 1957. (Will Gainfort Collection, Alexander Library Special Collections.)

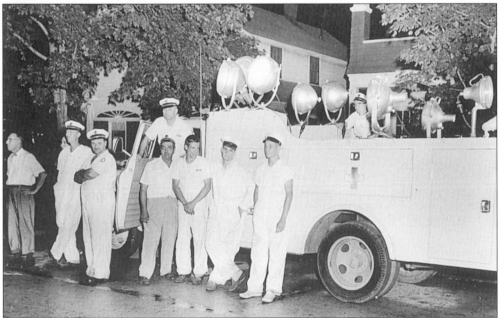

LIGHTENING UP THE NIGHT, 1961. First Aid Squad members and cadets stand beside their 1955 Chevrolet rescue truck. In addition to first aid calls, the squad responded to fires. The truck's spotlights were used to help light up the scene during night calls. Thanks for 50 years of service to the community. (Highland Park Volunteer Fire Department.)

A Reporter's Assignment, 1922. In January 1922, Elmer B. Boyd, publisher of the *Daily Home News*, challenged reporter G. Wallace Conover to "see what you can do about a library in Highland Park." Within 48 hours, Conover, assisted by Viola Jennings of the newspaper and Harry Benders, Boyd's chauffeur, established a library in the house at 9 North Second Avenue. Mrs. John T. Green, a retired teacher, served as volunteer librarian. Photographed here by C.C. Francis are, from left to right, William Skidmore (the building's owner), G. Wallace Conover, and Harry Bender. Boyd's library officially became the Public Library of Highland Park by a November 1922 referendum. The library later moved to the Masonic Building. In 1924, Bertha Skevington became the first full-time qualified librarian and held the job for 40 years. The Lucas property was designated a library and recreational site in 1955. Plans were drawn up by architect Ernest Levine and construction began in 1958. The new library's official dedication took place on July 4, 1959. (Highland Park Public Library.)

Seven

RELIGIOUS
ORGANIZATIONS

MEMBERS OF THE CHOIR, C. 1903. Reverend Edward J. Meeker and his choir pose for a photograph after rehearsal at the Reformed Church. (Reformed Church of Highland Park.)

A SUNDAY SCHOOL TEACHER, JANUARY 1897. Most cabinet photographs have no inscriptions on the backs of their mat boards. However, this one recounts the sad tale of Ella Van Schoick, a Reformed Church Sunday school teacher, who died when her house on South First Avenue near Raritan burned down. (Reformed Church of Highland Park.)

THE OLD SCHOOLHOUSE, THE NEW SUNDAY SCHOOL, 1908. The histories of the town and the Reformed Church are deeply entwined. The congregation started by meeting in the one-room schoolhouse; after its 1907 purchase for $37, the school was moved one-and-one-half blocks from the corner of South Second Avenue and Benner Street to become the Reformed Church's chapel and Sunday school. Along with the cost of moving and small renovations to the front, the ivy-covered church had a new building for just $62. It remained in use until the mid-1960s. (Borough of Highland Park Historical Commission.)

CHILDREN'S DAY FESTIVITIES, 1908. The Malmros family provided decorations for the Reformed Church's Children's Day, transforming the interior of the new Sunday school. After 1913, a larger chapel was constructed and this building was turned into a gymnasium that was then used by the entire community. (Reformed Church of Highland Park.)

A GROUP PORTRAIT, C. 1922. Dressed in their Sunday best, these Reformed Church congregation members posed for photographer Joseph De Maria. (Reformed Church of Highland Park.)

Baptist Chapel, Highland Park, N. J.

THE SECOND CHURCH, FIRST LOCATION, C. 1907. From 1893 to 1895, Baptists in Highland Park held prayer meetings at various homes. In 1895, a Sunday school organization met in a former grocery store. Paterson's farm lot, on Raritan Avenue at the corner of what would become North Second Avenue, was purchased in 1899 and the chapel seen here, designed by August N. Whitlock, was constructed. The building was finished in the spring of 1900 and dedicated on Sunday, June 3, 1900, in a ceremony that included addresses given by the area's clergy. (Carolyn Kuhlthau.)

THE SECOND CHURCH, SECOND LOCATION, 1966. Even after a 1911 expansion, the old Baptist chapel was outgrown by the late 1920s. Reorganizing in 1925 as the First Baptist Church of Highland Park, the congregation collected money for a building fund. On Sunday, December 7, 1930, the First Baptist Church, reconstructed from the old chapel, which had been moved 100 feet away from Raritan Avenue, was dedicated. An additional story was constructed under the old structure and covered with brick, as seen in this 1966 photograph by Joseph Koye. A planned Gothic Revival church on the lot fronting Raritan Avenue was never constructed. (Highland Park Historical Society.)

HIGHLAND PARK'S THIRD CHURCH, 1928. By 1910, Catholics in Highland Park who attended St. Peter's Church in New Brunswick started a movement for their own parish. Property at the corner of Raritan and South Sixth Avenues was purchased in 1912. Nearly a year after the cornerstone ceremony, on July 4, 1914, architect William Boylan's Gothic Revival-style church was blessed and dedicated by the Bishop of the Diocese. The building was known as the St. Paul's Chapel until the arrival of its first priest, Reverend Francis Quinn, in 1919, when it became the Church of Saint Paul the Apostle. Over the years, the church property expanded to include a rectory, convent, and school. (Church of Saint Paul the Apostle.)

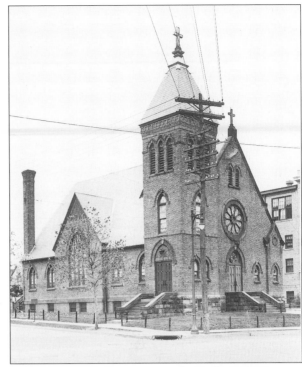

THE INTERIOR OF SAINT PAUL'S, 1951. This wedding ceremony photographed by Victor Gabriel shows the interior of St. Paul's before its major renovation, which doubled the size of the church in 1952. The architect, parishioner Harry Bach, died before the work was completed. (Church of Saint Paul the Apostle.)

THE INTERIOR OF THE GREEK ORTHODOX CHURCH, C. 1945. A Greek Orthodox congregation raised funds in several states to build the modest Saint George Church at 9 River Road in 1919. Its central location and accessibility by trolley from Perth Amboy and Trenton was a major factor in the choice of this site. Few people have seen its delicately carved iconostasis, which holds the paintings of various Christian saints. According to church doctrine, these images are to honor, not worship, the saints. The Greek congregation worshiped here until 1962, when they relocated to their present church in Piscataway. (St. George Greek Orthodox Church.)

THE SAME CHURCH, NEW CONGREGATION, C. 1970. The church building was transferred in March of 1963 and is now St. Mary's Russian Orthodox Church. Here, the congregation of the Byelorussian Autocephalic Church of Saint Mary of Zurovicy spills out of the church at 9 River Road and poses for a contemporary group portrait taken by South River photographer and parishioner Alex Silvanowicz.

A Confirmation Class, All Saint's Episcopal, 1935. The Reverend John Doberstine and a confirmation class pose before the pointed arch and heavy wooden doors of the All Saint's Episcopal Church on Magnolia Street at South Third Avenue. This church began as a mission in 1924, when a group of Highland Parkites held services in the Masonic Building and then purchased a house to be used as a church and rectory. William H. Leupp bequeathed $100,000 to the All Saints Mission, enabling the members to build a church. Ground was broken in the fall of 1926, and by November 1927 the church was completed. After a dedication ceremony on December 14, 1930, the Gothic Revival edifice (seen in a 1955 woodcut print below) was called "the prettiest little church in this part of the State." (Juanita Barlow Messer.)

THE GROWTH OF RELIGION, 1927. And you thought digging the garden was work! Early-20th-century building methods were still crude, but as the population of Highland Park soared, the need for residential properties and houses of worship increased. These men, hired by the general contractor Lewis Brothers of Highland Park, are digging a hole for the basement and foundation of the Trinity Methodist Episcopal Church on Montgomery Street. (Phyllis Loetzer.)

A STURDY FOUNDATION, 1927. Montgomery Street was well developed by 1927. The desirability of suburban life and close-knit but detached single family houses spurred a corresponding rise in municipal services. This decade saw the establishment of a public library and a police department. The new *Highland Park Press*, "covered the borough of homes like the sky above." Franklin Junior High School is visible in the background of this photograph, one of a series of Trinity Methodist Church construction snapshots taken by Cora Schenck. (Phyllis Loetzer.)

THE BUILDING TAKES SHAPE, 1928. Silhouetted construction workers erected the scaffolding necessary for constructing the pointed arch of the church's doorway. Just to one side of the arched entrance, the cornerstone was put into position during a ceremony in 1928 that featured esteemed members of the congregation. (Phyllis Loetzer.)

A MODIFIED GOTHIC DESIGN, 1928. Designed by Philadelphia architect George E. Savage, the Gothic Revival-style church was formally dedicated on June 3, 1928, with a set of three services at 10:30 a.m., 3:00 p.m., and 7:45 p.m. Fred Eayres, a contractor in Highland Park, built the brick parsonage next door to the church during the same year. (Phyllis Loetzer.)

RABBI ISADORE SHALOM RAVETCH AND PUPILS, 1932. Rabbi Ravetch was hired after the established group who started the Hebrew School organized into the Highland Park Conservative Temple and built a small temple at 109 North Third Avenue. It was dedicated in three days of festivities from September 12 to 14, 1930. Here the Rabbi poses with the following people, from left to right: (front row) his son Herbert, Beulah Kotis, and Blanche and Sidney Berkowitz; (back row) his son Irving, Marvin Susswein, Albert Davis, and Aaron Beck. (Ruth Patt and The Jewish Historical Society of Central New Jersey.)

THE HIGHLAND PARK CONSERVATIVE TEMPLE, C. 1949. The Jewish population increased rapidly in the 1930s and they soon outgrew their facility on North Third Avenue. In 1944, a committee was organized to raise funds for a new temple that was to include a recreation and education center. Property on the corner of South Third Avenue and Benner Street was secured and ground was broken in December 1948 for this contemporary synagogue of cast stone and brick designed by architect Ernest Levine. In solemn ceremonies on Sunday, September 18, 1949, the temple was dedicated in time for Rosh Hashonah, which began five days later. (Highland Park Conservative Temple.)

OPENING MASS AND BLESSING, 1950. Bishop Ahr presided over the mass and blessing of the Cenacle Retreat House on the day it opened, July 2, 1950. It was given to the Congregation of Our Lady of the Retreat in the Cenacle by Robert Wood Johnson Jr., in memory of his longtime friend James A. McGarry, whose daughter was a Religious of the Cenacle. As Johnson stipulated, a memorial mass commemorating McGarry's death takes place annually on March 6. (Sisters of the Cenacle.)

AN IDYLLIC RETREAT HOUSE, C. 1951. One of Highland Park's oldest houses is seen here from the air. At the entrance to this beautiful estate stands a driveway post with the inscription "Belleview." Since 1950, the Sisters of the Cenacle added a two-story wing on the back of the house and have sold off part of the land, but little else has changed. (The Sisters of the Cenacle.)

SEPHARDIC CONGREGATION ELDERS, 1960. On May 15, 1960, elder members of the Sephardic Congregation Etz Ahaim posed at the groundbreaking ceremony for their new building at 230 Dennison Street. They are, from left to right, as follows: (seated) Sam Ergas, Albert Amar, Jack Saltiel, and Daniel Cohen; (standing) Avram Saltiel, Solomon Auyash, Isaac Nahama, Solomon Arouh, Simon Auyash, and Haskiah Nifoussi. (Congregation Etz Ahaim.)

CONGREGATION ETZ AHAIM TEMPLE, 1963. The Sephardic community, made up of European immigrants who settled in New Brunswick in the early part of the 20th century, joined to form a congregation in 1927. Members of Congregation Etz Ahaim (Hebrew for Tree of Life) can trace their ancestry to the Sephardic Jews expelled from Spain in 1492. Formed in New Brunswick, the congregation built this contemporary structure designed by Englewood Cliffs architect Lowell Brody in Highland Park to replace their synagogue, which was demolished during one of New Brunswick's commercial plaza building campaigns. The synagogue was dedicated on March 24, 1963. (Congregation Etz Ahaim.)

Eight
WORK, PLAY,
AND CELEBRATIONS

THE ATLINSON FAMILY, 1905. Preparing for a pleasure trip in their Jackson touring car, the Atkinsons of 117 Benner Street pose for the camera. From left to right are Condit; his wife, Mary; his brother Frank; Condit Jr.; Mildred; and Lillian. (Borough of Highland Park Historical Commission)

THE BARTER, 1907. Thirteen-year-old Annie Elizabeth Page took her young nephew, Richard Page, for a stroll, while the baby's mother, Mary Mullen Page, finished making Annie's eighth grade graduation dress. Annie was the daughter of 1905 borough council member Charles P. Page; Richard was his grandson. (Pat Burns Toth.)

PARASOLS AND PETTICOATS, C. 1909. Parasols were carried to create shade on a hot summer day. How times have changed. Today's women wear shorts to keep cool! (Borough of Highland Park Historical Commission)

THE SPORTING LIFE, C. 1908. The Livingston Manor athletic field and clubhouse between Lawrence and Lincoln Avenues, seen on the 1910 Aero-View map on p. 29, were great gathering spots. They opened on May 31, 1909, and during the teens, Ray Brinkman ran summertime programs here. With the accouterments of croquet and baseball at their feet, these men posed in front of the clubhouse and appear ready to enjoy a sporting summer day. Even though it was located in Livingston Manor, the field was open to everyone. The children look ready for a game of autumn football in the photograph below. (Edgar donation to the Borough of Highland Park Historical Commission.)

THE BARLOWS AND GULICKS, 1911. On the porch at 40 South Fourth Avenue, two-year-old Juanita Barlow poses with her extended family, which included Aunt Hester B. Gulick, Uncle Bill Barlow, Gram Jennie Barlow, Uncle Clarence Gulick, Grandpop Gulick, Ethel H. Barlow (Juanita's mother), and Joseph H. Barlow (Juanita's father). (Juanita Barlow Messer.)

FIRE DEPARTMENT HORSEPOWER, 1911. Cornelius B. McCrelis, Highland Park's fire chief from 1914 to 1915, stands with a horse that was used to pull the fire department's 1899 hose cart until the first motorized fire truck was purchased in 1915. This photograph was taken in New Brunswick. (Highland Park Volunteer Fire Department.)

KIDS PLAY AND MOM WORKS, C. 1917.
Clementine and Juanita Barlow play in
their backyard at 128 Raritan Avenue
while Mrs. Senker babysits. Their mother,
Ethel Hardy Barlow, was an essential
partner of the family drugstore business,
especially during 1918, the year of the great
flu epidemic. Juanita would also help by
washing bottles and delivering
prescriptions on her scooter. (Juanita
Barlow Messer.)

SERIOUS MUSICIANS, 1923. Connie S. Atkinson Jr., fourth from the left, posed for this
publicity photograph along with the other members of his band. (The Atkinson Family.)

SCHULTZ FAMILY PHOTOS, C. 1925. Helen Schultz was photographed at Ayres Beach with her friends, Elizabeth and Helen. Schultz would later run a sweet shop in the same store that had been her father's grocery store. The oldest store in the area, Ignatz Schultz opened it in 1915 at 116 Woodbridge Avenue on the corner of Eleventh Avenue. In the snapshot below, Joseph J. Schultz, co-inventor of the portable salt box for keeping ice cream frozen, strikes a pose with his car in front of 216 Harper Street. (Gerard T. Schultz.)

A Boating Outing, 1927. The Rotarians enjoy a day on a boat. (Edgar donation to the Highland Park Historical Commission.)

Dad Bought a New Camera, c. 1920. Mother Lulu Woodward smiles at her happily bundled children, Mildred, age one, and Carl R. Woodward Jr., age three, in this photograph taken on their front lawn at 253 Lawrence Avenue. (Carl R. Woodward Jr.)

A Gala Event, 1922. The Raritan River has always been an ideal one for boating. In May 1892, the New Brunswick Boat Club was organized as a social group to "revive aquatic sport" that had been started by the Bachelor Boat Club in 1865. Over the years, regattas and water carnivals showcased national and even internationally known athletes. One such occasion, photographed by C.C. Francis, was held on Saturday, September 2, 1922. Over 10,000 onlookers lined the Albany Street Bridge, the canal towpath, and the riverbank. Boats of all

types formed a colorful lane for the swimmers. Fifteen-year-old Gertrude Ederle set a record in the 440-yard freestyle beating England's champion, Hilda James. This might have been the last swim meet, but the boat club continued to organize regattas. During a severe storm in 1927, the boathouse in the picture broke from its moorings at the bridge's third pier and floated down the river to land at Ayres Beach! The 40-year-old structure burned on December 28, 1933, and another was built in its place. (Borough of Highland Park Historical Commission.)

FROM THE REFORMED CHURCH ARCHIVES, C. 1925. Only a few people have been identified in this group portrait of young women from the Reformed Church of Highland Park. Helen Conover is third from the left in the back row and her sister Grace is eighth from the left. Betty Samson stands to the far left in the front row. (Reformed Church of Highland Park.)

KEEPING COMPANY, 1930. Theodore Pisciotta and Mary Myers dress in the latest fashions for an afternoon outing. The couple later married and became the parents of this book's co-author, Joanne Pisciotta, and Theodore Pisciotta Jr., Highland Park High School's track and field champion of the 1960s. (Joanne Pisciotta.)

TWO PARISHIONERS, 1937. Miss Cora Schenck and Mrs. Anna Rush of the Trinity Methodist Church enjoy the June sun. Miss Schenck, an original church trustee and Sunday school teacher, created the photographs documenting the building of Trinity Church seen in the previous chapter. (Phyllis Loetzer.)

RADIO DAYS, C. 1940. Auto mechanic and amateur radio operator Larry Caneel of 203 Cedar Avenue posed in his radio room. His transmitter is the large box to the left with his call letters on it. This photograph is one of Caneel's QSL cards, which he would send to verify contacts he made. The walls are covered with the QSL cards he received from other ham radio enthusiasts. (Highland Park Historical Society.)

A POLE VAULTER, 1940. Football was not the only game at the high school. Track and field, basketball, baseball, tennis, and soccer teams were available to high school boys. In 1940, the Girl's Athletic Club, a self-run extramural program, organized different sporting events such as volleyball, baseball, and basketball for girls. Several decades later, Title IX would require schools to provide equal expenditure on sports programs for boys and girls. (Borough of Highland Park Historical Commission.)

PLAIDS AND STRIPES, 1943. The Lafayette School Girl's Safety Patrol pose for a picture wearing dresses made from the popular stripes and plaids of the day. The girls helped the hallway monitors keep order inside the school and worked with the crossing guards to prevent accidents outside. (Bernice Bernstein Archive, Highland Park Historical Society.)

ROOM TO GROW, 1942. With Karsey Street in the background, the Schultz family line up with their vehicles in their large back yard at 211 South Eleventh Avenue. From left to right are cousin Joseph Egan, Joseph Schultz Jr., George, mother Catherine, and Jerry Schultz. (Gerard T. Schultz.)

"TO MOTHER AND DADDY," 1944. Amelia Augustono had this portrait made for her parents at New Brunswick's Dale Studios. She is one of five children from one of this century's first African-American families in Highland Park. She still lives in her childhood home. Fondly remembering walking to New Brunswick to attend high school in the 1930s, she stated that "it was a thrill each day because you got to see the water when crossing the bridge." An oil painting of Dr. Martin Luther King Jr. by this self-taught artist hangs at the King Center in Atlanta. (Amelia Augustono.)

GOING TO THE CHAPEL, C. 1947. A bride is on her way into St. Paul's Church in an early Joseph Koye picture from the collection of his nephew, Rich Odato.

A CHILD-FRIENDLY TOWN, 1948. There is no better holiday for children than Halloween! Dressed as their favorite characters, these Lafayette School students pose for a picture just before the annual Halloween parade, a tradition still practiced in the schools today. (Bernice Bernstein Archive, Highland Park Historical Society.)

CUB SCOUT PACK 55, C. 1949. Cub scout troops were sponsored by many organizations, including the churches and synagogues. Here, Pack 55 marches in a parade turning the corner from North Fifth Avenue onto Raritan Avenue. The Fifth Avenue Sweet Shop behind them was a popular teen hang-out after high school let out for the day. (Florence Fais.)

HIGH SCHOOL MAJORETTES, 1950. Looking sharp in their uniforms, two drum majorettes strike a pose for *Daily Home News* photographer Will Gainfort in front of Highland Park High School. (Will Gainfort Collection, Alexander Library Special Collections.)

THE REC, 1948. The borough's recreation department youth center in the basement of the Reformed Church was made possible through the volunteer efforts of dozens of civic-minded Highland Park residents. Formally opened on February 24, 1948, it was not long before hundreds of Parkites of all ages were using the center. It came to an end with a devastating New Year's Eve fire at the end of 1963 and beginning of 1964. The "Rec" relocated to a new building on Raritan Avenue by 1966. (Pat Burns Toth.)

THE KARSEY STREET PLAYGROUND, C. 1952. Fresh air and dappled sunshine greet these children as they swing at Karsey Street playground. The land was deeded to the borough specifically for use as a playground into perpetuity. (Pat Burns Toth.)

A CONFIRMATION CLASS, 1951. The Conservative Temple's confirmation class of 1951 poses for a photograph. By December 1964, the expanding congregation had its new addition next to the temple on South Third Avenue. The addition included more Hebrew School classrooms and a gymnasium. (Will Gainfort Collection, Alexander Library Special Collections.)

THE BEST VIEW, 1960. Cruising past the Highland Park Barber Shop on his way to the Presidency, John F. Kennedy waved at Christine Beck, the daughter of future mayor G. Paul Beck, who served from 1972 to 1976. Christine snapped this picture from the sidewalk in front of Saint Paul's Church. (Rose Mary Beck Murphy.)

Within the image:
Albany Street Bridge
New Brunswick
over Raritan River
Route 1 - M.P. 31.4
Widened & Rebuilt
1925
Picture 10-27-25.
Looking from
Highland Park
Toward
New Brunswick.

ON ITS WAY, 1925. A lone motorcar makes its way along Highland park's newly widened section of Raritan Avenue toward the Albany Street Bridge and beyond. (New Brunswick Free Public Library.)

Selected Bibliography

Center for Public Archeology. *Cultural Resource Reconnaissance Survey.* New Brunswick: Rutgers University, 1993.

Cultural Resource Consulting Group. *Livingston Manor District: Evaluation of Historical Significance.* Privately printed, 1997.

Highland Park Herald Special Report. "Highland Park's Heritage." Somerville, NJ: Forbes Newspapers, 1989.

League of Women Voters of Highland Park. "Our Towns." 1953.

———. "Know Your Town." 1959.

Rebarber, Ellen. *Reflections of Long Time Residents of Highland Park.* Highland Park: privately printed, 1998.

Shultise, Samuel J. *The Public Schools of Highland Park: 1885–1940.* Highland Park: privately printed, 1940.

Wright, Mary C. "An Informal History of Highland Park, New Jersey in the Years Since its Founding in 1905." New Brunswick: Rutgers University, 1976.

For a complete bibliography, please send a note along with a self-addressed, stamped business-size envelope to: Highland Park Historical Society, P.O. Box 4255, Highland Park, New Jersey, 08904.